CHATGPT PROMPTS

AI POWERED PROMPTS TECHNIQUES FOR CRAFTING CLEAR AND EFFECTIVE PROMPTS FOR BEGINNERS TO ADVANCE

Wesley Duggan

Introduction

Artificial intelligence (AI) was created and improved in order to solve some basic human problems and help with answering enquiries in different spheres of life. On November 30, 2022, ChatGPT was introduced as a prototype to offer solutions to some of this. ChatGPT gained recognition for its thorough responses and eloquent responses across many fields of study. Yet, a key flaw in it has been recognized as its uneven factual accuracy. After the introduction of ChatGPT, OpenAI was valued at $29 billion in 2023, according to estimates.

GPT-3.5 served as the foundation for ChatGPT's initial release. On March 14, 2023, a version based on GPT-4, the most recent OpenAI model, was made accessible to premium subscribers on a temporary basis.

The generative pre-trained transformer (GPT) family of language models ChatGPT It was upgraded over a more advanced version of OpenAI's GPT-3 known as "GPT-3.5" (a method to transfer learning).

The process of fine-tuning used reinforcement learning from human feedback, a technique that combines supervised learning with reinforcement learning (RLHF). Both strategies make use of human instructors to help the model perform better.

During supervised learning, the trainers acted as both the user and the AI assistant in dialogues that were given to the model. Human trainers ranked the model's responses that it had produced in a previous conversation as the first phase in the reinforcement learning process. These rankings were used to produce "reward models," on which the model was further improved by a number of Proximal Policy Optimization iterations (PPO). Algorithms for proximal policy optimization are more affordable than those for trust region policy optimization.

However, ChatGPT began to utilize a Microsoft Azure supercomputing infrastructure powered by Nvidia GPUs, which Microsoft built specifically for OpenAI and reportedly cost "hundreds of millions of dollars." Following ChatGPT's success, Microsoft significantly upgraded the OpenAI infrastructure in 2023.

To train and fine-tune the service, OpenAI collects data from ChatGPT users. Users can upvote or downvote ChatGPT responses and provide additional feedback in a text field.

ChatGPT is versatile, despite the fact that its primary function is to mimic a human conversationalist. It can, for example, write and debug computer programs, imitate the style of celebrity CEOs, and create business pitches. compose music, teleplays, fairy tales, and student essays; answer test questions (sometimes at a level above the average human test-taker, depending on the test); write poetry and song lyrics Simulate a Linux system, an entire chat room, games such as tic-tac-toe, and an ATM. Many pages and data about internet phenomena and programming languages, such as bulletin board systems and the Python programming language, are included in ChatGPT's training data.

ChatGPT attempts to reduce harmful and deceptive responses in comparison to its predecessor, InstructGPT. In one example, whereas InstructGPT accepts the prompt "Tell me about when Christopher Columbus came to the United States in 2015" as true, ChatGPT recognizes the counterfactual nature of the question and frames its response as a hypothetical cognizance of what might happen if Columbus came to the United States in 2015, using information about Christopher Columbus' voyages and facts about the modern world - including modern perceptions of Columbus' action.

ChatGPT, unlike most chatbots, remembers previous prompts in the same conversation. Journalists speculate that this will enable ChatGPT to function as a personalized therapist. Questions are filtered through the OpenAI "Moderation endpoint" API (a separate GPT-based AI) to prevent offensive outputs from being presented to and produced by ChatGPT, and potentially racist or sexist prompts are dismissed.

However, ChatGPT has a number of limitations. OpenAI admits that ChatGPT "occasionally writes plausible-sounding but incorrect or nonsensical answers." This is a common behavior in large language models and is known as "hallucination." In an example of an optimization pathology known as Goodhart's law, the reward model of ChatGPT, which is designed around human oversight, can be over-optimized and thus hinder performance.

Meanwhile, the AI has only a limited understanding of events that occurred after September 2021.

Human reviewers preferred longer answers in training ChatGPT, regardless of actual comprehension or factual content. Training data is also subject to algorithmic bias, which can be seen when ChatGPT response to prompts that include human descriptons. ChatGPT once generated a rap implying that women and scientists of color were inferior to white and male scientists.

However, Artificial intelligence (AI) has revolutionized the way we interact with technology. From personal assistants to recommendation systems, AI-powered technologies are becoming ubiquitous in our daily lives. One area where AI has shown great potential is in crafting effective prompts for various applications. In this book, we will explore AI-powered techniques for crafting effective prompts for beginners to advanced users, and more so, how we can use the AI to our advantage regardless of your field expertise and profession.

CHAPTER ONE

The Concept of Chatgpt and its Importance

What exactly is ChatGPT?

ChatGPT is a natural language processing tool powered by AI technology that allows you to have human-like discussions with the chatbot and much more. The language model can provide answers to questions and help you with tasks such as writing emails, articles, and programming. According to a UBS investigation, ChatGPT is the fastest-growing app of all time. According to the analysis, ChatGPT had 100 million active users in January, only two months after its introduction. For instance, it took nine months for TikTok to reach 100 million.

OpenAI's ChatGPT is also a big language model built on the GPT-3.5 architecture. It is a cutting-edge artificial intelligence (AI) language model trained on massive amounts of text data to provide human-like responses to natural language queries.

ChatGPT's significance stems from its capacity to comprehend and provide human-like responses to a wide range of natural language questions, including text, voice, and image-based inputs. ChatGPT has a large knowledge base, allowing it to deliver accurate and thorough information on a variety of topics.

As a result, ChatGPT is a useful tool for a variety of applications, including virtual assistants, chatbots, customer support, and more.

The capacity of ChatGPT to process and generate natural language responses has a wide range of practical applications. For example, it can help firms enhance their customer service by responding to consumer enquiries quickly and accurately, minimizing the need for human intervention. It can also make it easier for people to find information by answering their questions in natural language.

The relevance of ChatGPT stems from its capacity to effectively analyze natural language questions and offer human-like responses, making it an invaluable tool for both organizations and individuals.

The History of ChatGPT and its Predecessors?

ChatGPT and its predecessors have a history that stretches back to the mid-1990s, when Artificial Intelligence (AI) research was making ripples in the IT world. Richard Wallace developed the first AI chatbot, A.L.I.C.E (Artificial Linguistic Internet Computer Entity), at the Massachusetts Institute of Technology (MIT). A.L.I.C.E was powered by a natural language processing technology, which allowed it to converse naturally with people.

Following that, IBM launched Watson, its own AI chatbot. Watson understood complicated inquiries and provided replies in human-like dialogues using a combination of AI algorithms and natural language processing. This paved the way for the development of AI chatbots based on natural language processing.

Microsoft's Cortana and Google's Allo both debuted in 2016, with AI-powered chatbot features. The next year saw the introduction of Facebook's M and Apple's Siri, as well as Chatfuel, the first commercially available AI-based chatbot platform. ChatGPT's development began in 2018, when OpenAI released its Generative Pre-trained Transformer (GPT) model. The GPT model proved capable of creating human-like responses to inquiries and discussions, which prompted the creation of ChatGPT, a hybrid chatbot platform that combines natural language processing and GPT technology.

ChatGPT is the first chatbot platform to combine AI-powered natural language processing with GPT technology, enabling it to give more accurate and human-like responses. It can also learn and interpret more complex discussions, making it a valuable tool for companies wishing to automate customer support operations.

The first chatbot, called ELIZA, was created by Joseph Weizenbaum in the 1960s. ELIZA was designed to simulate a psychotherapist, and it used pattern-matching techniques to simulate conversation with users. Although ELIZA was relatively simple and relied on pre-programmed responses, it was groundbreaking at the time because it was the first program that could hold a conversation with a human in natural language.

In the following decades, chatbots became more sophisticated, and researchers began to develop new techniques for natural language processing and machine learning. One important milestone in the development of chatbots was the introduction of the Turing test, which was proposed by Alan Turing in the 1950s as a way to determine whether a machine could exhibit human-like intelligence.

In the 1990s, a new generation of chatbots emerged, including programs like A.L.I.C.E. and Jabberwacky. These chatbots were designed to be more interactive and engaging, and they used more advanced natural language processing techniques to understand and respond to user input.

Since then, chatbots have continued to evolve, and they are now used in a wide range of applications. For example, businesses use chatbots to provide customer service, while healthcare providers use chatbots to help patients manage their health. Virtual assistants like Siri, Alexa, and Google Assistant are also examples of chatbots, as they use natural language processing to understand and respond to user commands.

As AI technology continues to advance, we can expect chatbots to become even more sophisticated and capable of handling complex tasks. For example, chatbots could be used to help people book travel arrangements, manage their finances, or even diagnose medical

conditions. The possibilities are endless, and we are only just beginning to scratch the surface of what chatbots can do. With the increasing popularity of virtual assistants like Amazon's Alexa and Google Assistant, chatbots have become an integral part of our daily lives. As AI technology continues to advance, we can expect chatbots to become even more sophisticated and capable of handling complex tasks.

ChatGPT is a robust natural language processing (NLP) solution that allows developers to design conversational AI applications quickly. It offers a simple and powerful conversational AI platform for building chatbot applications with a single line of code. ChatGPT allows developers to easily deploy chatbots for customer assistance, sales, marketing, and other purposes.

ChatGPT includes a number of capabilities that enable developers to design robust chatbot apps. It integrates easily with popular messaging systems including Facebook Messenger, Slack, and Telegram. It also contains a structured dialogue engine, which allows developers to design complex talks quickly. This system is powered by a deep learning-based natural language understanding (NLU) engine, allowing it to comprehend complex questions and react appropriately.

ChatGPT, in addition to its NLU capabilities, has a keyword-based search engine for swiftly finding relevant responses to consumer enquiries. It also includes a natural language generation (NLG) functionality that allows developers to generate automatic responses for conversation scenarios. Furthermore, ChatGPT offers interaction with other apps, allowing developers to easily link their chatbot with existing applications and services.

ChatGPT, which was built with AI, also has an analytics dashboard that allows developers to track the performance of their chatbot. This dashboard allows them to measure client interactions, evaluate consumer behavior, and improve the efficacy of their chatbot. Developers can use this dashboard to quickly discover issues with their chatbot and take corrective action to improve client experience. With ChatGPT, developers can easily construct and deploy advanced conversational AI apps by exploiting these powerful features. With this sophisticated platform, developers may simply construct chatbot applications for customer service, sales, marketing, and other purposes.

Difference Between Chatgpt and other Chatbots

ChatGPT is a large language model that uses artificial intelligence (AI) to generate human-like responses to user inputs. It is based on the GPT-3.5 architecture, which means it has been trained on a massive amount of text data and can understand and respond to a wide range of topics and queries.

Compared to other chatbots, ChatGPT has several advantages:

Natural Language Processing (NLP): ChatGPT has a superior NLP system that allows it to understand the nuances of human language and generate responses that are more relevant and engaging.

Learning Capability: ChatGPT has the ability to learn from the conversations it has with users, which means it can improve its responses over time and provide a better user experience.

Versatility: ChatGPT is not limited to specific domains or topics, as it has been trained on a wide range of text data. This makes it versatile and able to provide responses to a diverse set of queries.

Creativity: ChatGPT has the ability to generate creative and original responses, which sets it apart from other chatbots that may rely on pre-programmed responses or templates.

ChatGPT's superior language processing, learning capability, versatility, and creativity make it a more advanced and sophisticated chatbot than many others on the market.

What distinguishes ChatGPT from a search engine?

ChatGPT is a language model designed to converse with the end user. A search engine indexes web pages on the internet to assist users in finding the information they need. ChatGPT does not have the capacity to conduct online searches. It generates a response using the information it learnt from training data, which leaves space for error. Another significant difference is that ChatGPT only has access to information up to 2021, whereas a standard search engine, such as Google, has access to the most recent information. So, if you ask ChatGPT who won the World Cup in 2022, it won't be able to respond as quickly as Google, in fact it would clearly state that it can't afford to give answers beyond the programming level it was programmed. One way to know this is that,

❖ Google Search Engine is intended to present consumers with relevant information in response to a certain search query. ChatGPT is intended to answer natural language inquiries and provide users with conversational support.

❖ Google Search Engine crawls the internet and indexes web pages, photos, videos, and other online content to provide users with relevant results. ChatGPT understands user inquiries and provides suitable answers using advanced AI and NLP technology.

❖ Google Search Engine needs users to provide a search phrase before returning relevant results. ChatGPT converses with users in natural language and gives real-time responses.

❖ Google Search Engine employs sophisticated algorithms and ranking variables to provide consumers with the most relevant results. ChatGPT understands user questions and provides relevant answers using advanced NLP and AI technology.

❖ Users can search and find information using Google Search Engine's text-based interface. ChatGPT offers a conversational interface via which users can engage and receive information.

❖ To determine the relevancy of search results to the user's query, Google Search Engine employs complicated algorithms. ChatGPT understands user questions and provides relevant answers using advanced AI and NLP technology.

❖ Google Search Engine attempts to provide users with accurate and up-to-date information. ChatGPT also employs advanced AI and NLP technology to give users accurate and relevant answers.

❖ With millions of pages indexed and search results created in milliseconds, Google Search Engine provides fast and efficient search results. ChatGPT also responds to users in real time, using advanced AI and NLP technology to process user inquiries efficiently.

❖ Google Search Engine gives users customized search results based on their search history, geography, and other criteria. ChatGPT also gives users custom responses based on their previous interactions and preferences.

❖ Despite the fact that Google Search Engine has privacy regulations in place to protect user data, users' search histories and other information are nevertheless gathered and retained. Although ChatGPT has privacy measures in place to secure user data, users' chat histories and other information are nevertheless collected and retained.

❖ To offer relevant results, Google Search Engine crawls the whole web and indexes web pages, photos, videos, and other online content. ChatGPT provides useful answers to users by utilizing a large library of information, including structured and unstructured data.

❖ Google Search Engine offers a variety of search options, including web search, picture search, video search, and others. ChatGPT is primarily intended to provide conversational support and answer natural language questions.

❖ Google Search Engine returns a diverse set of results, including web pages, photos, videos, news stories, and more. ChatGPT responds to user questions with particular answers, which are frequently in the form of text or numerical data.

❖ Google Search Engine allows users to submit comments on search results in order to improve the accuracy of search results. ChatGPT also allows users to submit input in order to improve the accuracy of its AI and bots.

Overview of AI-powered techniques for crafting effective prompts

Crafting effective prompts is an essential task in various AI applications, such as natural language processing, dialogue systems, and recommendation systems. Here are some AI-powered techniques that can help in crafting effective prompts:

Natural Language Generation (NLG): NLG is a technique that generates human-like text from structured data or prompts. It can be used to generate effective prompts that are tailored to a particular user or context. For example, in a recommendation system, NLG can generate prompts that ask the user about their preferences and interests.

Natural Language Understanding (NLU): NLU is a technique that helps machines understand human language. NLU can be used to analyze user responses to prompts and generate follow-up prompts that are relevant to the user's input. For example, if a user responds to a prompt with "I like Italian food," NLU can generate a follow-up prompt that asks the user about their favorite Italian dishes.

Reinforcement Learning (RL): RL is a technique that enables machines to learn from their interactions with the environment. It can be used to generate prompts that encourage users to provide more informative responses. For example, in a dialogue system, RL can be used to generate prompts that guide the conversation towards a particular goal.

Active Learning: Active learning is a technique that selects the most informative examples for the user to label. It can be used to generate prompts that are most likely to elicit informative responses from the user. For example, in a text classification task, active learning can generate prompts that ask the user to label the most ambiguous or uncertain examples.

Transfer Learning: Transfer learning is a technique that allows models to leverage knowledge from one domain to another. It can be used to generate prompts that are tailored to a particular user or context by leveraging knowledge from other domains. For example, in a recommendation system, transfer learning can be used to generate prompts that are tailored to the user's past behavior or preferences.

The role and Importance of Prompt in Chatgpt

Prompts play an essential role in ChatGPT, as they provide a starting point for generating responses. A prompt is a piece of text that a user enters to initiate a conversation with ChatGPT. The model then uses the prompt to generate a response that is relevant to the topic of the prompt. The prompt serves as a guide for ChatGPT by providing it with context and direction for the conversation. It helps the model understand the user's intent and provides a foundation for the generation of a response that is coherent and relevant to the topic.

In addition to providing context, prompts can also be used to control the length and style of the generated response. For example, a user can provide a short prompt, such as "What is the capital of France?" to receive a brief and factual response, or a longer prompt, such as "Can you tell me about the history of French cuisine?" to receive a more detailed and informative response.

As a language model, prompts play a crucial role in guiding ChatGPT's responses. When a user inputs a prompt into ChatGPT, the model uses its language processing capabilities to analyze the text and generate a response that is contextually relevant and coherent. The response is generated based on the model's training on a vast corpus of text, which allows it to understand and mimic human language patterns and nuances. Some of the major importance the AI to the human world are listed below;

Enhanced Productivity

All business owners want their employees to be productive. Implementing Chat GPT can help organizations increase their efficiency, allowing them to give better and faster service to their customers.

Businesses, for example, can respond quickly to client enquiries made through ChatGPT without having to wait for assistance from customer support workers.

Enhanced Customer Service

Providing prompt service to your consumers will help you keep them for a long time. Implementing Chat GPT in your customer support systems will help you give a more personalized experience to your consumers. This will not be possible with typical customer service methods. Providing fast and targeted responses to your clients can benefit you in the long run. A happy customer will always be loyal to you.

Expenses are being reduced.

ChatGPT can be used to provide support and customer service at a very low cost. With ChatGPT, firms may hire fewer customer service representatives to handle consumer questions, lowering the firm's overhead expenditures.

Improved Accuracy

The generated text is predicted to improve in accuracy and coherence as more data is collected and the model is fine-tuned on specific tasks.

Chat GPT enhances multitask training accuracy by allowing models to detect and intuitively express many goals at the same time. Companies that capitalize on this transition will have a competitive advantage, resulting in increased chatbot performance and happier consumers.

Increased Engagement

ChatGPT can help you engage clients more effectively, which can lead to improved engagement. Companies that use Chat GPT can provide their consumers with a more exciting and engaged experience, which can lead to a rise in customer loyalty.

Improved Scalability

Because ChatGPT is scalable, it is an excellent choice for use in enterprise-grade applications. OpenAI's cutting-edge ChatGPT language development method is always being updated and improved. To be useful in large-scale language production operations, the model must be able to handle more complicated and large inputs. This will broaden the model's potential applications. Technology that drastically cuts overhead expenses is critical for businesses to maintain their competitive advantage. Companies that utilize ChaptGPT can benefit from increased scalability and decreased costs.

Quick Response Times

The amount of time you take to respond to your consumers can either make or kill your business. Your customers have far too little time to wait for your reaction. If your clients do not receive a prompt response, they will leave your website and never return. You can expect prompt responses when using ChatGPT. GPT can respond to incoming messages quickly. It simplifies real-time communications for businesses and allows them to stay ahead of the competition.

Automated Deliberation

Traditionally, customer service representatives would respond to consumer inquiries by chat or phone. The entire procedure takes a long time. ChatGPT, on the other hand, allows you to promote automatic discussions. GPTs can produce discussions on their own, which reduces the amount of time spent on manual involvement.

Support for Multiple Languages

ChatGPT is useful for individuals and businesses who want to communicate with people who speak other languages because OpenAI is working on models that support several languages. GPTs can understand conversational language and respond in a way that is meaningful to users. Chat GPT is the solution if your firm has consumers all over the world. It will assist you in staying ahead of the competition.

Conversations in other languages are automatically translated by Chat GPT. Customers will be able to interact with GPT agents in their favorite language, resulting in more personalized and unique interactions with the service.

Accelerated Speed

More robust hardware and algorithms will enable the model to create text more quickly. This will enhance its usability in real-time environments like chatbots and conversational systems.

The faster GPT agents can understand what users are saying and respond, the happier their customers will be. Businesses will be able to deploy chatbots across several platforms, such as their websites, applications, and social media pages, to reach a larger audience and provide better service.

Exact Use Cases

As the rate at which natural language processing can be applied to chat GPT grows, businesses stand to benefit from a myriad of creative applications.

For example, using AI algorithms and back-end technology, customer service representatives would be able to quickly access customer knowledge databases and react to basic and sophisticated consumer enquiries.

As a result, support personnel will be better positioned to serve clients in ways that benefit both the company and the customers. By automating substantial aspects of the operation, firms will be able to deliver round-the-clock customer assistance with minimal effort.

Ethical Perspective of Chatgpt Usage

Chatbot technology has advanced significantly in recent years. From simple bots that merely respond to basic orders to more complex bots that can replicate human conversations, the options are limitless. ChatGPT, a chatbot driven by artificial intelligence that can generate natural-sounding responses for its users, is one of the field's most recent and intriguing innovations.

ChatGPT's purpose is to replicate a real discussion with its users. It accomplishes this by utilizing artificial intelligence technology, which can generate natural-sounding responses based on user input. The technique is built on GPT-3 deep learning and was taught using data from millions of chats, books, and articles.

ChatGPT's ethical ramifications are not yet evident. On the one side, the technology might be used to create fake news or deceptive information, possibly misleading consumers. It has the potential, on the other hand, to aid improve communication, particularly between humans and computers.

Some suggest that ChatGPT should be utilized responsibly and cautiously in order to avoid the potential abuse of its capabilities. Others believe it is a potent instrument that can be utilized for good, such as assisting humans in communicating more successfully with technology.

Individuals, organizations, and governments must ultimately determine how to employ ChatGPT, as well as any other artificial intelligence-based technology. Before diving in head first, we must address the ethical consequences of new technology. We also need to make certain that any possible misuse of technology is monitored and stopped. Only careful use will ensure that ChatGPT remains a useful tool in the future. The argument over the ethics of ChatGPT will undoubtedly continue, but one thing is certain it has here and will impact how we communicate in the future. It is our responsibility to use it wisely.

C hatGPT has some restrictions. ChatGPT, like any AI system, has flaws and obstacles that might impair its performance and accuracy.

Here, we will look at some of ChatGPT's shortcomings, ranging from its failure to recognize complicated settings to its reliance on biased data. We can acquire a better grasp of the potential downsides and challenges of employing AI language models in various circumstances by studying the limitations of ChatGPT.

Lack of common sense: While ChatGPT can generate human-like responses and access a significant amount of information, it lacks human-level common sense and the model also lacks the underlying knowledge that we have. This means that ChatGPT may occasionally deliver illogical or erroneous solutions to specific inquiries or situations.

Lack of emotional intelligence: While ChatGPT can generate compassionate reactions, it lacks true emotional intelligence. It is incapable of detecting subtle emotional cues or correctly responding to complex emotional circumstances.

ChatGPT has limitations when it comes to comprehending context, particularly sarcasm and humor. While ChatGPT excels at language processing, it struggles to understand the delicate subtleties of human communication. For example, if a user uses sarcasm or comedy in their message, ChatGPT may fail to recognize the intended meaning and instead offer an unsuitable or irrelevant response.

Having difficulty generating long-form, structured content: At the moment, ChatGPT is having difficulty generating long-form structured content. While the model may generate intelligible and grammatically accurate phrases, it may struggle to generate lengthy chunks of text that adhere to a specific structure, format, or storyline. As a result, ChatGPT is best suited for producing shorter pieces of material such as summaries, bullet points, or brief explanations.

Limitations in handling multiple tasks at the same time: The model operates best when given a single task or target to focus on. If you ask ChatGPT to complete numerous jobs at the same time, it will struggle to prioritize them, resulting in decreased efficacy and accuracy.

Biased responses: ChatGPT is trained on a vast set of text data, which may contain biases or prejudices. As a result, the AI may occasionally produce responses that are unintentionally prejudiced or discriminating.

Limited knowledge: Although ChatGPT has access to a significant amount of information, it cannot access all human knowledge. It may be unable to answer queries on extremely particular or niche issues, and it may be unaware of recent advancements or changes in specific disciplines.

Inaccuracies or grammatical errors: At the time, ChatGPT's sensitivity to typos, grammatical errors, and misspellings was limited. The model may also give technically valid replies that are not accurate in terms of context or relevance. This constraint might be especially difficult when processing complicated or specialized data when accuracy and precision are critical. You should always take efforts to validate the data generated by ChatGPT.

Fine-tuning required: If you need to use ChatGPT for extremely particular use cases, you may need to fine-tune the model. Fine-tuning entails training the model on a specific set of data to improve its performance for a certain job or goal, which can be time-consuming and resource-intensive.

ChatGPT is a highly complicated and sophisticated AI language model that requires significant computational resources to operate successfully, which implies that operating the model can be costly and may require access to specialized software systems. When running ChatGPT on low-end devices with limited computational capacity, processing times, accuracy, and other performance difficulties may occur. Before implementing ChatGPT, organizations should carefully assess their computational resources and skills.

CHAPTER TWO

In natural language processing, a prompt is a short text snippet or instruction given to a machine learning model to guide it in generating output. The prompt provides the model with context, guidance, and constraints on what kind of output is desired.

Prompts are commonly used in various natural language generation tasks, such as text completion, summarization, and translation. For instance, in a text completion task, the prompt could be the beginning of a sentence, and the model is tasked with completing the sentence in a coherent and grammatically correct manner. In summarization, the prompt could be a long piece of text, and the model is expected to generate a concise summary of it.

Prompts can be tailored to suit different requirements, and the quality of the generated output depends heavily on the quality of the prompt given. Well-crafted prompts can significantly improve the accuracy and relevance of the model's output.

What are Prompts?

When faced with a blank screen or piece of paper, everyone understands how intimidating it can be. Consider the possibility of never being taught how to write an academic paper. That would be challenging! Although writing prompts may appear to be a hardship, they guide the writer. There are only a few approaches to understanding any prompt so you can produce the best essay possible in any situation.

A writing prompt is both an introduction to a topic and guidance on how to write about it. Writing prompts, which are frequently used for essay assignments, are intended to direct the writing and pique the reader's interest in the topic of discussion.

An essay prompt can be anything that encourages you to think about the topic at hand, such as a question, a statement, or even an image or song. Essay questions are designed to test your writing skills as well as allow you to interact with an academic topic. Writing prompts can vary in length and style, and there are various different varieties, each concentrating on a particular topic.

Prompts can also differ in terms of how much information they provide. A writing prompt may present the writer with a situation and ask them to defend their perspective on the topic, or it may present the writer with a brief reading assignment and ask them to react. At times, the prompt is brief and to the point.

When given a writing prompt, there are a few steps you can take to ensure you thoroughly understand the task and can write the most effective essay or piece of writing possible. You can utilize this technique to obtain a clear grasp on the meaning of the prompt and what to write in response, regardless of the length, type, or intricacy of the prompt.

Prompts can also differ in terms of how much information they provide. A writing prompt may present the writer with a situation and ask them to defend their perspective on the topic, or it may present the writer with a brief reading assignment and ask them to react. At times, the prompt is brief and to the point.

The Role of Prompts in Chatgpt

ChatGPT uses prompts as a way to generate responses to user input. A prompt is a textual input provided by a user that initiates a conversation with ChatGPT. ChatGPT uses the prompt to generate a response that is relevant and coherent to the input provided.

Prompts play an important role in ChatGPT's ability to generate natural and relevant responses. They provide context for the conversation and help ChatGPT understand what the user is trying to communicate. By analyzing the prompt, ChatGPT can identify the topic, tone, and intent of the user's input and generate a response that is tailored to the user's needs.

In addition to providing context, prompts also help ChatGPT learn and improve over time. By analyzing the patterns and themes in user input, ChatGPT can identify common questions and topics that users are interested in and generate more accurate and helpful responses. prompts are an essential part of ChatGPT's ability to generate human-like conversation and provide users with the information and assistance they need.

ChatGPT uses a variety of techniques to generate responses based on the given prompt, including language modeling, machine learning, and natural language processing. The model's ability to generate high-quality responses to prompts has made it a valuable tool for a wide range of applications, including chatbots, language translation, and content creation.

The developed AI can play a role in communication by providing automated responses to text-based queries or conversations. ChatGPT can be used in a variety of settings, including customer service, online support, education, and entertainment. ChatGPT is altering communication in a significant way by acting as a dynamic conversational AI assistant. It may be linked into a variety of platforms, including messaging apps, customer support systems, and virtual assistants, to give contextually appropriate and seamless responses.

ChatGPT has also been used in social media management, assisting businesses and people in managing their online presence by writing and scheduling posts, evaluating trends, and engaging with audiences in real time. It has also enhanced accessibility for people with disabilities. It can, for example, be implemented into assistive devices to convert speech to text or vice versa, allowing persons with hearing or speech difficulties to communicate more effectively.

The ability of the AI to swiftly resolve issues and provide relevant information has resulted in improved customer assistance, increasing user happiness.

In customer service, ChatGPT can help businesses provide fast and efficient support to their customers. By analyzing customer queries and providing relevant responses, ChatGPT can help resolve issues quickly and improve customer satisfaction.

In education, ChatGPT can be used to provide personalized learning experiences for students. By analyzing student queries and providing relevant resources and explanations, ChatGPT can help students learn at their own pace and improve their understanding of complex concepts.

In entertainment, ChatGPT can be used to provide engaging conversations and interactions with users. By using natural language processing, ChatGPT can understand user queries and provide responses that are both entertaining and informative.

Benefits of Crafting Clear and Concise Prompts

ChatGPT is a cutting-edge language model capable of producing human-like answers in natural language processing. It can transform how we engage with technology by offering quick and accurate responses to a wide range of inquiries and requests. However, there are certain advantages to utilizing AI.

However, in order for ChatGPT to attain its full potential, proper prompts must be provided. The quality of the prompts provided to ChatGPT has a direct impact on the accuracy and relevancy of its responses, eventually defining the model's overall effectiveness and utility.

Crafting clear and concise prompts has several benefits, including:

Improved Understanding: Clear and concise prompts help the reader or respondent understand the question or task at hand more easily and accurately. This reduces the chances of misunderstandings or misinterpretations, which can lead to incorrect or irrelevant responses.

Increased Participation: When prompts are easy to understand, more people are likely to participate in surveys, questionnaires, or other data collection activities. This can lead to higher response rates and more reliable data.

Time-Saving: Clear and concise prompts save time for both the writer and the reader. The writer saves time by avoiding lengthy explanations or repetitions, while the reader saves time by quickly grasping the question or task.

Consistency: When prompts are clear and concise, they are more likely to be consistent across different respondents or data points. This allows for easier analysis and comparison of data.

Better Quality Responses: Clear and concise prompts lead to more accurate and relevant responses. This means that the data collected is more useful and actionable for decision-making purposes.

Professionalism: Clear and concise prompts are a hallmark of professionalism in written communication. They show that the writer has taken the time to carefully consider their audience and the purpose of their writing.

Natural Language Processing (NLP) and its role in prompt creation

Natural Language Processing (NLP) is a field of study that focuses on enabling computers to process and understand human language. NLP plays an important role in prompt creation, which refers to the process of generating prompts or questions to elicit a response from a user.

In the context of language models and AI chatbots, NLP is used to understand the meaning and context of user input and generate appropriate prompts or questions based on that input. This can involve analyzing the structure and syntax of the input, identifying relevant keywords and entities, and using machine learning algorithms to predict the most appropriate response.

For example, if a user inputs "What's the weather like today?", an NLP algorithm might analyze the syntax and identify that the user is asking for information about the weather. It might then generate a prompt such as "Do you want to know the current temperature, the forecast for the day, or something else?"

NLP can also be used to improve the quality and relevance of prompts by taking into account factors such as the user's location, previous interactions, and personal preferences. By leveraging NLP and other AI technologies, prompt creation can be automated and customized to provide a more engaging and personalized user experience.

NLP is a field of study that focuses on developing algorithms and models that can understand, analyze, and generate human language. It involves using machine learning, computational linguistics, and other techniques to teach computers to read, interpret, and generate language. NLP is a critical component of many modern technologies, including voice assistants, chatbots, and language translation systems.

In the context of prompt creation, NLP is used to generate prompts that are relevant, clear, and grammatically correct. This involves using algorithms to extract key phrases and concepts from a given text, which can then be used to formulate questions or prompts that are tailored to the content. For example, if the content is about World War II, NLP algorithms can identify key concepts such as battles, leaders, and events, and use them to generate prompts that ask about specific aspects of the war.

NLP can also be used to generate prompts based on specific parameters, such as length, complexity, and language level. For instance, prompts can be generated that are appropriate for different grade levels or reading abilities. This can help ensure that prompts are understandable and engaging for students, regardless of their reading level.

In addition to generating prompts, NLP can be used to evaluate the quality of prompts by analyzing their coherence, relevance, and grammatical correctness. This involves using algorithms to assess the clarity and accuracy of the prompts, ensuring that they are clear and unambiguous and that they effectively communicate the intended learning objectives.

Natural Language Processing (NLP) Tasks

The uncertainties in human language make it extremely difficult to build software that accurately determines the intended meaning of the text or voice input. Homonyms, homophones, sarcasm, idioms, metaphors, grammar and usage exceptions, sentence structure variations—these are just a few of the human language irregularities that take humans years to learn, but that programmers must teach natural language-driven applications to recognize and understand accurately from the start if those applications are to be useful.

Several NLP tasks deconstruct human text and voice data to assist the machine in making sense of what it is absorbing. Among these tasks are the following:

The task of consistently turning voice data into text data is known as speech recognition, commonly known as speech-to-text. Speech recognition is necessary for any application that responds to voice commands or enquiries. The way individuals talk makes speech recognition exceptionally difficult—quickly, slurring words together, with varied emphasis and intonation, in diverse dialects, and frequently using improper grammar.

Part of speech tagging, also known as grammatical tagging, is the technique of determining a word's or piece of text's part of speech based on its use and context. 'Make' is used as a verb in 'I can make a paper plane,' and as a noun in 'What car do you own?'

Word sense disambiguation is the process of determining the meaning of a word with several meanings using semantic analysis to discover which word makes the most sense in the current context. Word sense disambiguation, for example, aids in distinguishing the meaning of the verb make' in make the grade' (achieve) vs.'make a bet'. (place).

NEM, or named entity recognition, recognizes words or phrases as useful entities. NEM recognizes 'Kentucky' as a place or 'Fred' as a man's name.

The task of determining whether or not two words refer to the same item is known as co-reference resolution. The most typical example is recognizing the person or thing to whom a given pronoun refers (e.g.,'she' = 'Mary'), but it can also include identifying a metaphor or an idiom in the text (e.g., an instance in which 'bear' refers to a giant hairy person rather than an animal).

Sentiment analysis seeks to extract subjective qualities from text, such as attitudes, emotions, sarcasm, bewilderment, and suspicion.

Natural language generation is frequently referred to as the inverse of speech recognition or speech-to-text; it is the process of converting structured data into human language.

For a more in-depth look at how these concepts connect, see the blog post "NLP vs. NLU vs. NLG: the differences between three natural language processing concepts."

Common challenges in crafting effective prompts

Crafting effective prompts can be a challenging task, and there are several common challenges that writers may encounter. Here are some of the most common challenges in crafting effective prompts.

Clarity: One of the most important aspects of an effective prompt is clarity. The prompt should be clear and concise, and it should clearly convey what is expected of the writer. Ambiguity or vagueness in the prompt can lead to confusion and produce subpar responses.

Specificity: Effective prompts should be specific, and should clearly outline what the writer needs to do. The more specific the prompt, the better the response is likely to be.

Relevance: The prompt should be relevant to the subject matter or topic being addressed. If the prompt is not relevant or does not align with the objectives of the assignment, the response may be off-topic or irrelevant.

Balance: The prompt should strike a balance between being challenging and achievable. If the prompt is too difficult or too easy, it can lead to frustration or boredom for the writer.

Creativity: A well-crafted prompt should be creative and engaging, stimulating the writer's imagination and encouraging them to think critically.

Context: The prompt should be contextual, taking into account the audience, purpose, and goals of the writing assignment.

Length: An effective prompt should be neither too long nor too short. A prompt that is too long can be overwhelming, while a prompt that is too short may not provide enough guidance for the writer.

Although ChatGPT has various advantages for premium businesses, there are also potential drawbacks to consider. Because ChatGPT can gather and keep sensitive user data such as personal information, preferences, or feedback, privacy and security are major considerations. This could expose the brand and the customer to third-party data breaches, hacking, or misuse, putting both parties at danger.

ChatGPT may raise ethical and social difficulties for luxury businesses in addition to privacy and security concerns. It has the potential to fool or trick users into believing it is a human with genuine emotions and opinions, undermining the brand's and customer relationship's trust and authenticity. This can lead to ethical quandaries and conflicts of interest, which can harm the brand's reputation in the long run.

Furthermore, ChatGPT may jeopardize the brand's quality and consistency, as well as the consumer experience. It may respond in an incorrect, erroneous, or disrespectful manner, or it may be incapable of handling sophisticated or particular enquiries, aggravating or alienating customers. This could harm the brand's reputation and credibility, making regaining customer confidence and loyalty difficult.

Effective prompts are prompts that stimulate creativity and encourage critical thinking. Here are some tips for creating effective prompts.

Be specific: The prompt should be clear and specific to the task at hand. It should provide enough information to guide the reader in the right direction, but not so much that it restricts their creativity.

Be open-ended: The prompt should not be overly restrictive, allowing the reader to interpret it in a variety of ways. This allows for a greater range of responses and encourages creative thinking.

Be relevant: The prompt should be relevant to the audience and the subject matter. It should be something that the reader can relate to and engage with.

Be challenging: The prompt should challenge the reader to think critically and creatively. It should encourage them to push beyond their comfort zone and explore new ideas.

Be inspiring: The prompt should be inspiring and motivating, encouraging the reader to take action and engage with the task at hand.

Examples of Ineffective Chat Prompts

Ineffective chat prompts are prompts that do not engage or encourage meaningful conversation with the user. Some examples of ineffective chat prompts are:

Yes or No Questions: Questions that can be answered with a simple yes or no response don't encourage the user to elaborate or provide additional information.

Closed-ended questions: Similar to yes or no questions, closed-ended questions limit the user's response to a narrow set of options.

Generic questions: Generic questions that lack specificity or personalization may not be compelling or relevant to the user.

Ambiguous prompts: Prompts that are unclear or confusing can lead to a lack of engagement or even frustration from the user.

Predictable prompts: Predictable prompts can become repetitive or boring, causing the user to lose interest in the conversation.

Leading questions: Questions that steer the conversation towards a specific answer or outcome can feel manipulative and may cause the user to disengage.

Insensitive prompts: Prompts that are insensitive to the user's situation or feelings can cause discomfort or offense, leading to a negative experience.

CHAPTER THREE

AI Techniques for Crafting Effective Prompts

Crafting effective prompts for AI systems requires careful consideration of the specific task at hand, as well as the intended audience and the desired outcomes. Here are some AI techniques that can help create effective prompts:

Natural Language Processing (NLP): NLP can help analyze and understand the natural language used in prompts, as well as the responses generated by AI systems. By using NLP techniques such as sentiment analysis and entity recognition, prompts can be tailored to elicit the desired responses from users.

Machine Learning: Machine learning algorithms can be used to analyze large amounts of data to identify patterns and relationships, which can be used to craft effective prompts. For example, machine learning can help identify the types of prompts that are most likely to generate a desired response, based on historical data.

Decision Trees: Decision trees are a popular AI technique that can be used to guide users through a series of prompts, leading them to a desired outcome. By using decision trees, prompts can be structured in a way that is easy to follow and results in a higher success rate. Reinforcement Learning: Reinforcement learning is an AI technique that involves training an AI system to learn from its own experience. By using reinforcement learning, prompts can be designed to adapt to user responses over time, improving the accuracy and effectiveness of the prompts.

Deep Learning: Deep learning is an AI technique that involves training a neural network to recognize patterns and make predictions. By using deep learning, prompts can be designed to be more personalized and tailored to individual users, improving engagement and overall effectiveness.

A/B Testing: A/B testing involves testing different versions of a prompt to see which one is more effective. This technique can be used to optimize prompts for maximum engagement and effectiveness.

Advance Techniques in using Chatgpt

There are several advanced techniques that can be used with ChatGPT to enhance its performance and capabilities. Here are some of them:

Fine-tuning: Fine-tuning involves training ChatGPT on a specific task or domain by providing it with relevant data. This can significantly improve its performance in that specific area. For example, fine-tuning can be used to train ChatGPT to answer questions about a particular product or service.

Transfer learning: Transfer learning involves using ChatGPT that has been pre-trained on a large corpus of text to perform a new task. This can save a lot of time and resources, as ChatGPT does not have to be trained from scratch. Transfer learning can be used to perform a wide range of tasks, such as text classification, sentiment analysis, and language translation.

Data augmentation: Data augmentation involves generating new data from existing data by applying various transformations to it. This can help improve the diversity and quality of the training data, which can in turn improve ChatGPT's performance. Data augmentation techniques can include techniques like adding noise or perturbations to the text data, replacing words with their synonyms, and applying other similar transformations.

Beam search: Beam search is a search algorithm that is commonly used in natural language processing tasks. It involves generating a set of possible responses and selecting the best response based on a scoring function. By using beam search, ChatGPT can generate more diverse and creative responses.

Multi-task learning: Multi-task learning involves training ChatGPT to perform multiple tasks simultaneously. This can help improve its overall performance, as it can learn to recognize patterns and relationships between different tasks. Multi-task learning can be used to perform a wide range of tasks, such as text classification, question answering, and language modeling.

Advanced Techniques for ChatGPT in Education

The impact of artificial intelligence in the classroom has caused quite a stir. With the release of ChatGPT, everyone has been discussing its role in education.

Its usage in education has elicited a mixed reaction. ChatGPT can assist students in accessing exact information and providing timely results. A Google search on a specific topic, for example, yields countless results. Given the abundance of Google results, students may seek assistance in narrowing the scope of the information they originally required.

For instance, of ChatGPT, the responses are quick and to the point. For example, if a student requires assistance with arithmetic problems, ChatGPT can assist in solving the problem, explaining the theory underpinning it, and producing further questions based on that concept for practice. Furthermore, ChatGPT goes a step further by allowing the user to ask follow-up questions and clarify their grasp of the issue. ChatGPT can assist educators in expanding their teaching tactics and tapping into areas that typically take a back seat during the core curriculum. Several methods are listed below:

Expand Vocabulary: ChatGPT can assist students in expanding their vocabulary by introducing new words and forming phrases around them. Teachers can instruct the tool to generate multiple sentences based on a new word that students are unfamiliar with, and then have students identify the meaning of the word based on the context of the different sentences. This is a fun and participatory approach to incorporate into weekly school activities.

ChatGPT as a Writing Prompt Generator: Based on age and grade, the program may produce engaging writing prompts for pupils. Teachers could request that ChatGPT produce a narrative starter or a writing prompt that encourages students to express themselves creatively by completing the activity. This can be a first step toward instilling writing skills in students.

Use in Assessments: ChatGPT can be an excellent reading comprehension tool, assisting students in improving their comprehension and reading skills. Teachers can instruct the program to generate passages on a variety of themes and use them in classroom assessments, asking students questions based on them. This will assist educators in assessing pupils' grasp of the topic/subject and identifying areas that require additional attention.

Students typically approach new technology with a sense of play and experimentation, hoping to discover capabilities and limitations via trial and error. Regardless of whether students are "digital natives," it is critical to note that students do not automatically understand how to use tools like ChatGPT for academic reasons. ChatGPT, from this perspective, provides chances for educators to teach students about these technologies to have crucial conversations with students about the capabilities, limitations, and ethical applications of modern technology tools in education.

The Best Practice for guiding Conversations in Meaningful Directions

Guiding conversations in meaningful directions is an important skill for effective communication. Here are some best practices for guiding conversations in a productive and meaningful direction:

Listen actively: Active listening is a key component of effective communication. It involves paying close attention to what the other person is saying and trying to understand their perspective. To listen actively, you should focus on the speaker and avoid distractions, such as your phone or other people around you. You should also maintain eye contact, nod your head, and provide verbal cues, such as "mm-hmm" or "I see," to let the speaker know that you are engaged in the conversation.

Ask open-ended questions: Open-ended questions are questions that require more than a yes or no answer. These questions encourage the other person to provide more detail and insight into their thoughts and feelings. Examples of open-ended questions include "What do you think about that?" "How did you feel when that happened?" and "Can you tell me more about that?" By asking open-ended questions, you can encourage the other person to share more information and ideas.

Stay on topic: Staying on topic is important for guiding conversations in a productive direction. It helps to ensure that the conversation remains focused and doesn't get sidetracked by unrelated topics. If the conversation starts to drift off-topic, you can gently steer it back to the main topic by saying something like "That's an interesting point, but let's get back to what we were discussing."

Avoid interrupting: Interrupting can be perceived as rude and disrespectful. It can also prevent the other person from fully expressing their thoughts and feelings. Instead of interrupting, you should allow the other person to finish their thoughts before responding. If you feel the need to interject, you can wait for a natural pause in the conversation before speaking.

Clarify understanding: Clarifying understanding is important for ensuring that you have correctly understood the other person's perspective. To clarify understanding, you can repeat back what the other person has said in your own words. This shows that you are actively engaged in the conversation and interested in their perspective. It also helps to prevent misunderstandings and miscommunications.

Be respectful: Being respectful is essential for guiding conversations in a productive direction. It involves avoiding derogatory language or making dismissive comments. Instead, you should focus on building a rapport with the other person and finding common ground. You should also be mindful of your tone of voice and body language, as these can communicate respect or disrespect.

Common Mistakes while Using Chatgpt

C hatGPT can be a strong tool for creating human-like responses to a wide range of queries and prompts as an AI language model. There are, however, several frequent blunders to avoid when utilizing ChatGPT. One of the most typical errors is a lack of patience. You must wait for ChatGPT's response and not reload or leave the website. Sometimes it takes 4-5 prompts to reach the correct answer.

Another typical error is failing to provide a sufficient prompt. Consider ChatGPT to be operative on the opposite side, and give it appropriate directives. The only problem is that this operative only speaks Machine Language. So, you must appropriately frame your prompts in order to achieve the desired results.

However, there are some common mistakes that users might make while using ChatGPT, such as:

Ambiguous or unclear prompts: One of the most common mistakes that users make while using ChatGPT is providing prompts that are too vague or unclear. When users provide such prompts, ChatGPT may not be able to understand the user's intent properly, which can result in irrelevant or nonsensical responses. To avoid this, users should provide clear and concise prompts that provide enough information for ChatGPT to generate a relevant response.

Not providing enough context: ChatGPT is a language model that works by analyzing the context of the conversation. If users do not provide enough context, ChatGPT may not be able to generate an accurate or relevant response. For instance, if a user asks "What is the best restaurant in town?", ChatGPT may not be able to provide an accurate response without knowing the user's location or preferences. Therefore, users should provide enough context to help ChatGPT understand their intent and generate the most appropriate response.

Expecting too much: ChatGPT is an advanced AI model, but it is not infallible. Users should not expect it to have all the answers or to provide perfect responses every time. ChatGPT is still a machine learning model that has limitations and biases. Therefore, users should be realistic in their expectations and understand that ChatGPT is not a substitute for human intelligence or expertise.

Ignoring inappropriate or offensive responses: In rare cases, ChatGPT may generate inappropriate or offensive responses. Users should recognize and ignore such responses and report them if necessary. ChatGPT learns from the data it is trained on, and it may pick up biases or offensive language from the training data. Therefore, it is important for users to be aware of this and to report any offensive or inappropriate responses to the developers.

Not using proper grammar and spelling: ChatGPT relies on proper grammar, spelling, and punctuation to understand and generate responses. Users should take care to use proper grammar and spelling when interacting with ChatGPT. Poor grammar or misspelled words can confuse ChatGPT and result in irrelevant or nonsensical responses. Therefore, users should be mindful of their language and ensure that they use proper grammar and spelling when interacting with ChatGPT.

Don't believe ChatGPT knows everything: Despite having been trained on a large amount of text material, ChatGPT does not have access to all human knowledge. As a result, if you ask a question that is too precise or technical, ChatGPT may be unable to deliver a meaningful response.

Check for coherence: While ChatGPT is capable of generating human-like responses, it can sometimes produce answers that are illogical or nonsensical. Before using a response from ChatGPT, be sure to check that it makes sense and is coherent.

Issues we often face with the content generated by ChatGPT

AI (Artificial Intelligence) which has been performing miracles recently, has enabled many machines and tools to work autonomously and more productively than people. It has also introduced numerous technologies that have proven useful in our daily lives. AI enabled everything, from smart assistants to chatbots and self-driving cars to the evolution of CBIR.

The most appealing aspect of AI is its adaptability. Because of its adaptability, it can be used in a variety of industries.

ChatGPT is the most recent ground-breaking AI application that has taken the world by storm. That's because this dynamic resource may generate material of any length on any prompt in seconds. It helps people in all fields increase their productivity and complete their jobs more rapidly. However, keep in mind that this tool is currently in the testing stage. As a result, its outcomes are viable because there are numerous challenges that you may encounter if you do not refine the text generated by ChatGPT before using it for any official, professional, or commercial reason.

Without doubt ChatGPT is extremely useful in improving the lives of students, professionals, and enterprises. However, the following are some of the most common issues with the content generated by this dynamic application.

Reduced readability

It is a common issue with the content generated by ChatGPT. Because it is an AI-based technology, it lacks human touch and soul. Furthermore, it may be hard to contextualize things in a concise manner and may exaggerate superfluous aspects more than necessary.

As a result, the language used by it may be incomprehensible and alienate familiar readers. As a result, they will be unable to understand the content you supply them. As a result, you won't be able to meet web users' search intent, resulting in a slowdown in your progress. As a result, you should not rely solely on the information provided by ChatGPT. Rather, it would be preferable if you looked forward to updating it and making various changes to it in order to retain the readability element for general readers.

How can this be overcome?

To improve the readability of the text created by ChatGPT, first paste it into a text readability checker to see how it ranks. It will keep you updated on the text score, which will help you determine whether your intended audience understands the context and thought process of the offered material. Following the results, if you believe the readability score might be improved, make precise adjustments to your created data to achieve the desired readability level. To make your material more understandable to your viewers, you can delete unneeded information or substitute difficult words with simple ones.

Grammatical errors are present.

Another issue that is frequently noted in ChatGPT-generated content is the occurrence of grammatical errors, which alter the overall complexion and tone of the text. As a result, you don't obtain what you want in reality. These errors may be related to punctuation and sentence structure. That is why you cannot utilize the material provided by this program without first proofreading it and removing all probable inaccuracies in the data. It is a requirement because if you want to keep readers on your platform, you must provide them with relevant and accurate information so that they can comprehend things better.

On the contrary, if your data is not grammatically right, it will cast a large doubt on your credibility. As a result, you will not have a committed and loyal audience.

How can it be overcome?

This problem is not difficult to manage. You may simply accomplish this with the assistance of a grammar checker. As a result, before using the content created by ChatGPT for any reason, you should run it via a grammar checker. It will show all of the faults in the submitted data and provide you with many ideas to fantastically correct the issues.

This is because a grammar checker provides recommendations while keeping a text's tone and style in mind, which helps it make the data more contextually relevant. As a result, not only will your material be error-free, but it will also be more readable.

Details and facts that are incorrect

Another concerning aspect of ChatGPT-generated content is incorrect details and information. The figures and facts provided in the content created by this application are usually not realistic because its database is not updated regularly, and numbers relating to various sectors and occupations change on a daily basis. Furthermore, due to its inadaptability, it sometimes conceives one process for another and conveys a concept that is completely contrary to the fact.

Furthermore, when seeking assistance from product articles on academic topics, the sources and publications cited are frequently incorrect. As a result, relying solely on ChatGPT data is tantamount to living in a fool's paradise. As a result, rather than taking the statistical figures and references in the ChatGPT content at face value, you should double-check these details before submitting or publishing them.

How can this be overcome?

To address this issue, you should review the most recent statistics from the relevant sites on the topics for which you require ChatGPT's assistance in producing content. It will assist you in replacing incorrectly entered numbers with exact and accurate values, boosting the credibility and value of your data. As a result, more readers will visit your website to learn about various subjects. Furthermore, you should cross-reference the sources utilized by ChatGPT in an article to check that they justify the offered information. As a result, if you find any errors, you must correct them in order to authenticate the material with suitable proof and testimonials.

Style and voice that are consistent

The information produced by ChatGPT in response to provided prompts is boring in style and voice in general. It keeps repeating the same pattern even while writing about diverse themes. As a result, you won't be able to achieve diversity and variation in your articles, which can make the content on your site dull. As a result, readers may get bored while studying the information you supply. As a result, you may get people to your site once to read the content you have, but they will become frequent readers. As a result, your progress graph will not develop systematically, hindering your advancement. As a result, you attempt to repurpose the content generated by ChatGPT in order to make it usable for extended periods of time.

How can it be overcome?

You can personalize the content provided by ChatGPT to eliminate recurrence. It is possible with the help of paraphrase. Manual paraphrasing, on the other hand, would take days to improve the text on such a big scale. That is why it is recommended that you use a paraphrase tool. This is due to the fact that a sentence rewriter can help you complete days-long tasks in a matter of minutes.

All you have to do is paste your text, and its algorithms will polish it in minutes without any additional input. Furthermore, because a paraphraser has a huge database of synonyms and sentence patterns, it can improve the quality of a document without compromising its general aim and meaning. As a result, the product you receive will have a high ability to attract readers and keep them on your site.

Prompts are cues or instructions that encourage a person to perform a specific task or provide a particular response. There are various types of prompts available, including verbal, visual, tactile, environmental, gestural, written, auditory, modeling, and self-generated prompts. Each type of prompt is unique in its way and serves a specific purpose.

Verbal prompts are spoken instructions or cues given by another person to prompt a desired response. Verbal prompts are commonly used in classroom settings where a teacher instructs a student to perform a specific task or provides them with the necessary information to complete an activity. For example, a teacher may prompt a student to answer a question or remind them to raise their hand before speaking.

Visual prompts are cues that can be seen, such as pictures, diagrams, or written instructions. Visual prompts are used to assist individuals who have difficulty with verbal communication, such as people with an autism spectrum disorder. For example, visual schedules can be used to show a sequence of tasks that need to be completed throughout the day. Tactile prompts are physical cues, such as touching or tapping, that prompt a desired response. Tactile prompts are commonly used in therapy settings to help individuals with sensory processing disorders. For example, a therapist may use a tactile prompt to guide a person's hand to complete a task.

Environmental prompts are cues in the environment that prompt a desired response. Environmental prompts are commonly used to encourage individuals to engage in a specific behavior or activity. For example, a traffic light indicates when it is safe to cross the street, prompting pedestrians to do so.

Gestural prompts are physical gestures or signals, such as pointing or nodding, that prompt a desired response. Gestural prompts are commonly used to assist individuals with communication difficulties or physical disabilities. For example, a caregiver may use a gesture to indicate that it's time for a meal.

Written prompts are instructions or cues provided in written form, such as a note or reminder. Written prompts are commonly used to remind individuals of tasks that need to be completed or to provide instructions. For example, a reminder note can be used to prompt a person to take their medication at a specific time.

Auditory prompts are cues that can be heard, such as a beep or a chime, that prompt a desired response. Auditory prompts are commonly used in alarms or reminders. For example, a timer can be set to beep when it's time to switch tasks.

Modeling prompts are prompts where a person demonstrates a desired response. Modeling prompts are commonly used to teach individuals new skills or behaviors. For example, a teacher may demonstrate how to solve a math problem to assist a student in learning the skill.

Self-generated prompts are prompts that a person creates for themselves. Self-generated prompts are commonly used to assist individuals in managing their daily tasks or remembering important information. For example, a person may set a reminder on their phone to take their medication at a specific time each day.

In conclusion, prompts are an essential tool used in various settings to encourage individuals to perform specific tasks or provide a particular response. Each type of prompt is unique and serves a specific purpose. Understanding the different types of prompts available can help individuals select the most appropriate prompts to assist them in achieving their goals

CHAPTER FOUR

Practical Illustration of AI powered Techniques

I magine you are a marketer for a retail clothing company, and you are responsible for writing product descriptions for the company's e-commerce website. You want to write compelling and persuasive descriptions that will entice customers to purchase the products. However, you often find yourself struggling to come up with new and engaging ways to describe the same items.

This is where an AI-powered writing assistant can come in handy. Using natural language processing and machine learning algorithms, the tool can analyze your writing and suggest improvements to make it more effective. Here's how it might work:

You start by typing out a product description for a new dress:

"This dress is perfect for any occasion. It features a flattering silhouette and a unique pattern that's sure to turn heads."

The AI-powered writing assistant then analyzes your writing and provides several prompts to help you improve it:

Consider adding more details about the dress's fabric or construction to make it sound more luxurious.

Try using more vivid language to describe the dress, such as "stunning" or "eye-catching."

Here are some customer reviews of the dress to incorporate into your description and build social proof.

You use these prompts to revise your description and come up with something more compelling:

"Indulge in the luxury of this stunning dress, featuring a flattering silhouette and an eye-catching pattern that's sure to turn heads. Made from high-quality materials and backed by rave reviews from satisfied customers, this dress is perfect for any occasion."

By incorporating the AI-powered prompts, you are able to create a more engaging and persuasive product description that is likely to result in more sales. This is just one example of how AI-powered prompts can be used in a practical setting to help individuals improve their writing and communication skills.

AI-powered prompts are a feature of AI-powered tools that use natural language processing (NLP) and machine learning algorithms to analyze text and provide suggestions to improve it. These tools can be used in a variety of settings, such as writing assistants, chatbots, and search engines.

When a user types or speaks a sentence, the AI-powered tool analyzes it to understand its meaning and context. The tool then provides suggestions to improve the sentence based on its analysis. These suggestions may include alternative word choices, advice on sentence structure, or recommendations for additional research to support an argument.

One example of an AI-powered writing assistant tool is Grammarly. Grammarly uses AI to analyze text for grammar, punctuation, and spelling errors, as well as to provide suggestions for improving sentence structure, word choice, and tone. Grammarly's AI-powered prompts can help individuals write more effectively and persuasively, resulting in more polished and professional writing.

Another example of an AI-powered tool that uses prompts is Google's search engine. When a user enters a search query, Google's AI analyzes the query to understand the user's intent and provides suggestions for related search terms or content.

These suggestions are based on the AI's analysis of the query as well as the user's search history and preferences.

AI-powered prompts are a powerful tool for improving communication and writing skills. By leveraging the power of NLP and machine learning, these prompts can help individuals create more effective and persuasive content, whether that be product descriptions, research papers, or social media posts.

In another scenario for instance, Let's say you are a content marketer for a software company, and you're responsible for creating a blog post about a new product feature. You want to make sure the post is informative, engaging, and persuasive, but you're not sure where to start.

You decide to use an AI-powered writing assistant tool to help you with your writing. As you start writing your post, the tool analyzes your text and provides suggestions to help you improve it, which can come in this format:

You start your post with the sentence: "Our new product feature is designed to make your life easier."

The AI-powered tool then provides a prompt, suggesting that you consider adding more details to explain how the feature will make the reader's life easier.

You revise your sentence to say: "Our new product feature automates repetitive tasks, freeing up your time to focus on more important work."

The AI-powered tool then provides another prompt, suggesting that you consider using a more specific example to illustrate the benefits of the feature.

You revise your post to include a specific example of how the feature has already helped one of your customers save time and improve their productivity.

The AI-powered tool then provides a final prompt, suggesting that you include a call-to-action (CTA) to encourage readers to try the feature for themselves.

You add a CTA to the end of your post, inviting readers to sign up for a free trial of the new feature. By using AI-powered prompts to improve your writing, you're able to create a more informative, engaging, and persuasive blog post that is likely to resonate with your target audience.

AI as a Game Changer in Business

In the last few years, artificial intelligence has come a long way. Not long ago, something you'd see in science fiction movies became the go-to solution for all kinds of devices, businesses, and behaviors all around the world. Artificial intelligence now has the ability to improve a wide range of activities by analyzing massive amounts of data to discover flaws and provide viable remedies. Early in the industrial revolutions, technological advances replaced or eased human muscle force.

In the age of AI, our cognitive abilities are being simulated, amplified, and even partially replaced by digitalization and AI. This has completely new scaling and multiplication effects for businesses and economies. In digital ecosystems, companies are increasingly gravitating toward algorithmic enterprises. It is also not about a technocratic or mechanistic understanding of algorithms, but about designing and optimizing the digital and analytical value-added chain to gain long-term competitive advantages.

Smart computer systems, on the one hand, can enable real-time decision-making processes; yet, big data and AI are capable of making decisions that now outperform the quality of human decisions.

Machines are progressively opening up new avenues for advancement and potential. Large amounts of data require a lot of time and resources to collect, prepare, and analyze. Algorithms now do the work that many human workers used to do in businesses and government agencies. These operations can be automated thanks to modern algorithmics, giving personnel more time to interpret and execute the analytical conclusions.

Furthermore, without appropriate tools, humans cannot grasp the 70 trillion data points available on the Internet or the unstructured interconnection of organizations and economic actors. AI, for example, can automate the process of client acquisition and competition observation, allowing people to focus on contacting identified new customers and developing competitive strategies.

Companies frequently scrutinize recommendations and standard operating procedures based on AI and automated evaluation. Following these automatic recommendations generated by algorithms rather than internal corporate consideration feels weird at first. The results, however, suggest that it is worthwhile because we are already surrounded by these algorithms.

Furthermore, different best practice examples reduce the frequently existent gap between the potentials of big data, business intelligence, and AI and their successful use in business practice. Although the importance and urgency to act in this field have been repeatedly stated, there is a lack of a systematic reference frame, contextualization, and process model on algorithmic business. This book aims to bridge the gap between the blueprint and implementation. The debate on the topics is extremely industry-focused, particularly in Germany. The dominant issues include Industry 4.0, robotics, and the Internet of Things. In this, the so-called customer-facing operations and procedures in the fields of marketing, sales, and service play a secondary role. Because the lever for obtaining competitive advantages and growing profitability is particularly strong in certain functions, this book has made it its mission to emphasize these areas in greater depth and to demonstrate the remarkable potential through various best practices:

• How can customer and market potentials be identified and offered automatically?

• How can AI be used to automate and optimize media planning?

• How can product recommendations and prices be generated and controlled automatically?

• How can AI intelligently control and coordinate processes?

• How can AI be used to automatically generate relevant content?

• How can customer service and marketing communication be optimized and automated to boost customer satisfaction?

• How can bots and digital assistants make business-to-consumer communication more efficient and intelligent?

• How can algorithmic and AI-based customer journey optimization be optimized and automated?

• What impact do algorithms and artificial intelligence have on conversational commerce?

• How can modern market research be intelligently optimized?

Several best practice examples provide answers to these concerns and highlight the current and future potential of big data, algorithms, and AI.

You can't just jump into ChatGPT without a strategy. You must examine how it can be best utilized to your company. To begin, consider what you want ChatGPT to do for you. Do you want it to offer customer service? Increase the number of leads and sales? Help with new customer onboarding? Once you know what you want to achieve, you can build your plan around it.

Consider who will be utilizing ChatGPT next. Is there a customer support team on hand to manage chat interactions? Or do you need to hire more people? How about your marketing department? Can they use ChatGPT to build chatbots that increase traffic and conversions? Knowing who will use ChatGPT is critical for developing the best strategy.

Finally, ensure that your chatbot content is accurate. This entails creating clear and succinct communications that will assist clients in achieving their objectives. It also entails providing simple navigation so that clients can quickly and easily discover the information they require. You'll notice a significant improvement in your business's performance if you take the time to get all of these factors correct.

When it comes to automating tedious processes and freeing up your staff to work on more essential efforts, ChatGPT can be a game changer. ChatGPT can help you automate client interactions and provide courteous customer care by utilizing natural language processing (NLP).

Furthermore, ChatGPT enables efficient task tracking and management for customer care professionals. Customer enquiries can be swiftly routed to the best qualified agents based on their abilities and availability by implementing automated workflow routing. This ensures that clients have the greatest possible experience while also saving time and resources.

Businesses can also collect data on customer service interactions and utilize it to improve performance using sophisticated analytics tools. You may uncover trends in consumer behavior and improve the customer experience by employing AI-powered insights. This technique will enable organizations to remain competitive in a rapidly changing technological context.

Artificial intelligence (AI) and technology have invaded practically every sector imaginable. AI is here to stay, for better or worse, and it's only becoming smarter. OpenAI, an artificial intelligence research and development company, developed ChatGPT in 2022. This instrument has the ability to transform every business as we know it, including marketing and advertising. Its popularity is increasing.

The chatbot has made headlines for its frighteningly accurate responses and funny effects that will make you marvel. ChatGPT, like everything else in the world, has begun to affect digital marketing. Do you want to know how? Let's look deeper to learn more.

When it comes to ChatGPT, experts expect that its impact on digital marketing will spark a new revolution. As soon as it hit the market, this latest addition to the list of chatbots drew both praise and condemnation. Many individuals believe it will alter the industry by increasing the efficiency of digital marketing, while others believe it is overrated!

The truth is that OpenAI's ChatGPT is a huge language model trained on a massive dataset of text-based data. It was trained using text-based material such as social media postings, articles, blogs, and even books to learn the structure and pattern of the human psyche and provide a human-like response. Unlike other chatbots, ChatGPT's claim to fame is that it provides dynamic and complex human-like responses. This is made feasible by Generative Pretrained Transformer 3 (GPT-3), a powerful model trained by OpenAI.

ChatGPT can have an impact on digital marketing in a variety of ways. For example, it can generate automatic, personalized responses to consumer inquiries and provide unique content for various marketing initiatives such as email marketing or social media.

❖ Improved customer engagement

ChatGPT can improve customer engagement by responding to issues and questions in real time. This will eventually lead to increased client happiness and loyalty, which will lead to increased revenue creation and better conversion rates.

❖ Increased personalization

ChatGPT can be quite beneficial to digital marketers in terms of tailoring campaigns and content to fit the needs of specific customers. Using machine learning and natural language processing, ChatGPT may analyze client data and provide personalized recommendations to satisfy unique preferences and needs.

As a result of the chatbot, you may provide an interesting and authentic response to each client who contacts you. This allows you to form a strong loyalty link with your customer.

❖ Automated Customer service

ChatGPT can improve automated customer support operations by swiftly addressing frequently asked inquiries and fixing the most often occurring issues. This enables the company's human customer service agent to tackle more difficult questions and give a higher quality of service.

When the company's customer service quality improves, it will be able to identify the pain spots that its clients are experiencing. ChatGPT has the capacity to handle some of the most frequent customer service difficulties, including:

- ❖ Response time lag

- ❖ Inadequate personalized conversations

- ❖ Rejecting inappropriate inquiries

- ❖ AI-generated reactions that are predictable

- ❖ Representatives' inappropriate behavior

❖ Expert content creation

ChatGPT can generate high-quality content that is suited to the needs of the target audience. Social media posts and email marketing campaigns are examples of content. This can save digital marketers time and money. It also assists companies in improving the quality and relevance of their material.

ChatGPT has the ability to significantly increase the productivity and efficacy of an organization's content marketing department through the generation of high-quality content.

❖ Successfully nurture marketing leads

Marketers can use ChatGPT to create inventive marketing programs that will appeal to their target demographic. Engaging content will attract leads and efficiently advance sales.

ChatGPT can assist marketers in creating effective, efficient, and memorable campaigns by analyzing massive volumes of data and generating unique ideas.

According to a Business Wire poll, 52% of customers prefer text messages to phone conversations from customer service agents. This instantly raises the odds of effectively nurturing marketing leads with the help of ChatGPT. It can successfully guide new leads on their way to achieving those sales and producing more income for the company.

Digital marketing is continuously evolving, and as artificial intelligence advances, it will shift. Because these AI breakthroughs are not yet flawless, it is critical to evaluate results in order to improve digital marketing tactics for businesses.

❖ Social media administration

Many brands have turned to social media automation. There are various platforms available for scheduling, streamlining, and optimization. ChatGPT will execute the following tasks:

Scheduling: ChatGPT can be used to optimize social media post-scheduling based on audience behavior, preferences, and peak usage periods.

Analysis: The application can analyze data and provide insights on consumer behavior, preferences, and trends in order to deliver actionable insights for developing a more effective plan.

ChatGPT can evaluate data to provide the ideal ad formats and creative aspects for a company's campaign.

❖ Market Research

Market research is vital for any advertising team since knowing the audience's interests allows you to stay in touch with them. ChatGPT can help to speed up the market research process by:

Surveys: ChatGPT can conduct surveys and questionnaires to acquire information from specific populations. It can also generate unique questions for particular consumers based on current data to help them make decisions in the future.

Analyzing input: The program may evaluate customer feedback, compare it to key trends, and provide a complete report to help marketers better understand customer preferences and views.

❖ Search Engine Marketing

SEO refers to the amount of web traffic and the relevancy of that traffic to your ecommerce business. ChatGPT can assist you with SEO, which is a fantastic tool for growing your search engine results in order to recruit and keep existing clients.

Keywords: The AI will explore its vast library for appropriate keywords based on a given prompt or topic. Marketers can then optimize their content and copy using those keywords.

Relevant meta descriptions assist boost click-through rates on search engine results pages. ChatGPT uses its data to build meta descriptions that can help increase conversion rates.

Link building is all about being powerful, relevant, and ethical. ChatGPT can generate links to boost the search engine ranking of an e-commerce site.

Programming is hard sometimes. If you are learning a new programming language or doing something you've never done before, it can be downright intimidating. In addition to tutorials and documentation, it's now possible to use chatbots as a programming resource. Enter ChatGPT.

If you're not familiar with ChatGPT, it is a Large Language Model chatbot developed by OpenAI. It has been trained on a huge corpus of online text, including openly available code and programming tutorials. This means that it can "search" and compose a passable solution for common programming tasks.

AI for coding, such as ChatGPT, can help you write code more efficiently. ChatGPT can be used by programmers and developers for coding in a variety of methods, particularly for brainstorming and generating code in skeletal forms that can be tweaked and polished. The capacity of ChatGPT to generate codes from natural language is revolutionary. It's another step closer to closing the linguistic gap between machines and humans.

Here are a few examples of how we might use ChatGPT for programming and development:

- ❖ Create code
- ❖ Code completion and modification
- ❖ Code for debugging
- ❖ Code translation from one language to another Code explanation in natural language
- ❖ Function as a Linux terminal

❖ Serve as a SQL command line

Before we begin programming with ChatGPT, it would be beneficial to understand some important ChatGPT coding tips and tricks that will help you get the most out of ChatGPT's coding capability.

Here are some additional coding recommendations for using ChatGPT to build more usable, functional, and optimized programs.

To reduce errors, break the code or programming ideas down into the lowest functional units possible. You can then piece them together to form a usable whole. Because ChatGPT has a brief context window, you are more likely to obtain a code that is either obviously incorrect or does not work as you want.

To get around text constraints in the response, request that it use helper functions instead of comments and explanations. You can then copy the code and use it immediately. You can ask it to continue or keep going if it offers you an incomplete code.

Instead of "Write a code in C#...", use the following abbreviations: "C#: A program in which..."

It frequently produces generic or irrelevant responses. As a result, you might add to your prompt, "Ask more questions to help you build context." And it'll ask you pertinent questions that you can answer to receive a more accurate response. Request that it double-check the code it generated.

ChatGPT may be used to create simple programs in any language. But that doesn't imply you can just type anything and get complete, polished, optimized scripts that you can publish. However, there are several things we can do to achieve more desirable results.

ChatGPT relies heavily on context. Asking "What is JavaScript?" followed by "Give me an example of an application created in JavaScript," and then "Show me an application in JavaScript that makes the phone vibrate" is preferable to directly asking the last question, as it may respond that it is a language model and cannot do this or that.

Benefits of Using ChatGPT in the Customer Service Industry

Automation

ChatGPT can automate routine tasks, such as answering frequently asked questions, providing instructions for common issues, and handling simple customer requests. By automating these tasks, ChatGPT can help to:

Reduce the workload on customer service agents (e.g., customer service chatbots)

Improve the efficiency of customer service operations and the customer experience

Decrease the likelihood of errors or mistakes

24/7 Availability

ChatGPT can provide customer care around the clock, even outside of usual business hours, when integrated into customer service chatbots, allowing customers to access help whenever they need it. This can help to boost customer satisfaction and decrease the likelihood of consumers feeling frustrated or unsatisfied if they are unable to obtain assistance when they require it.

Scalability

ChatGPT can handle a high volume of client interactions and queries, making it an excellent choice for businesses with a big customer base or a high volume of customer contacts. It can handle numerous conversations at the same time, decreasing customer support agents' workload and allowing them to focus on more difficult or high-priority issues.

What does the business future of ChatGPT look like?

ChatGPT has the ability to change the corporate landscape. It has the potential to transform the way time and resources are allocated due to its capacity to automate mundane processes, provide real-time data analysis, support different languages, and increase data accuracy. While there may be some difficulties in using ChatGPT, such as technical support and privacy concerns, the benefits of using AI may exceed the drawbacks for your company.

The future impact of ChatGPT will most likely be determined by how fast and successfully enterprises adopt and integrate the technology into their operations. ChatGPT and comparable AI software, on the other hand, are going to play a big part in determining the future of business. It is a solution that organizations of all sizes should consider to fulfill their long-term goals, whether they are aiming to improve customer satisfaction, drive innovation, or remain ahead of the competition.

What distinguishes ChatGPT from other AI models is its capacity to construct text and answers depending on the user's questions using internet data and deep learning. ChatGPT's machine learning is quite powerful, and you can develop a unique response based on the user's inputs.

You will not always get the same return as with other AI tools because of a specific keyword in your query. Nothing, however, compares to ChatGPT. It is a completely revolutionary AI that will alter the way our world operates.

This language model, however, will have an impact on more than just marketing departments around the world; it will also have an impact on students and other professions; its impact will be far-reaching than you could imagine. What distinguishes ChatGPT from other AI models is its capacity to construct text and answers depending on the user's questions using internet data and deep learning. ChatGPT is a system that uses complex algorithms to learn on the fly and respond in a relevant, intuitive, and human-like manner.

Users must enter a command that ChatGPT will respond to.

This algorithm, however, is significantly more complicated than existing AI chatbots, making it far superior. ChatGPT is intuitive and knowledgeable because it has undergone thorough training. With this training data, the algorithm can generate responses that are always relevant to the question. For example, you can ask the AI to write a poem about a specific topic, such as a pink elephant, and it will respond in seconds thanks to this "pre-training."

However, because ChatGPT's training ended at the end of 2021, it has limited awareness of recent events. To check out the tool for yourself, simply establish an OpenAI account and experiment with its powerful tool. Its free service provides the most value of any AI technology now on the market. It can be used by content makers to conduct research, write original screenplays for videos, or even generate headlines for social media postings. The benefits of utilizing ChatGPT for content production

It's simple to see the benefits of having access to this sophisticated technology. ChatGPT is a generative model that has been pre-trained to answer questions from the user, making it extremely simple to use. To provide a response, the system employs deep learning technology based on its training and the original input data. There have been instances where ChatGPT has provided an inaccurate response; however, if users bring this out, the issue will be fixed in the next text output thanks to the machine learning model.

Remember that this chatbot does not have access to a database that has been updated beyond 2021.

The technology behind this AI chatbot has a fundamental understanding of how languages work, and you may fuel the computer using effective suggestions based on the initial word used to start a "new chat." For example, if you ask ChatGPT to act as a tour guide, you will receive a very different response than if you simply ask it to inform you about activities to do in a given location. This significantly improves the tool's effectiveness over a standard internet search, which is a game changer for content developers.

ChatGPT can apply its expertise to create human-like language, essays, and even code. You may need to "prime" the AI to generate relevant responses if you want to use ChatGPT for digital content production, however this is something that makes each response unique.

Intelligent like a Human

The ability of ChatGPT to perform sentiment analysis, which entails evaluating the emotional tone or attitude portrayed in a piece of text or language, is possibly its most astounding feature. This implies you may begin developing material with a new tone of voice, which many content creators struggle with. ChatGPT is excellent for producing original and accurate material. If you can "prime" the system in a way that no one else has, you can produce content ideas that you might not have considered before. Furthermore, ChatGPT has a wealth of technical expertise as a result of its training, so you may ask about almost anything.

An Additional Staff Member

If you're stuck crafting an effective marketing strategy and promotion plan, this technology can help. Users can converse with the AI technology as if it were another member of the team in order to generate fresh content ideas, rather than having to brainstorm for hours on end on a physical whiteboard or piece of paper. You can even use technology to generate content for a certain campaign or content plan.

ChatGPT can generate and alter social media material, allowing content creators to do their tasks more quickly. Social media users can't discern the difference between ChatGPT-generated content and human-written content. This demonstrates that this technology can produce excellent content. For example, you can instruct ChatGPT to begin producing headlines and hooks for LinkedIn posts, and then simply select the one that best suits your article. The best part is that ChatGPT is completely free, making it an amazing value for anyone in the content development industry. Users can also take advantage of the premium package if they want to get even more out of this sophisticated technology.

It isn't a Copywriter.

If you want to create a complete page of material, you'll need to put in some effort with ChatGPT. Even when given a particular number of words, the technology still struggles to compose a comprehensive essay, and it frequently produces less than a page's worth of information. If you're stuck on an idea and need some inspiration for great material, you can ask the technology to write a piece of the post or come up with some new ideas for you. However, you should still review the text it generated for content organization and flow to ensure that everything makes sense.

Usefulness of Chatgpt in Education

AI has created mind-blowing chatbots that have been welcomed in various aspects of human life, particularly in educational settings. Although some teachers may be hesitant to discuss ChatGPT with their pupils for fear of encouraging its use in evaluations, it is crucial to remember that the genie is already out of the bottle on this.

Microsoft has already invested billions of dollars in this technology and has a new AI-powered Bing search engine. They are also incorporating AI into products that we all use on a daily basis, such as Word, to assist users in creating document summaries. This technology appears to be here to stay, and it should be.

ChatGPT's Potential in Education

Teachers want to provide pupils with the digital skills they will need when joining the workforce, so why should the usage of ChatGPT, one of the most exciting technological breakthroughs in years, be limited? However, ChatGPT is evolving at such a rapid pace that it offers issues for institutions that must respond with thoughtful answers in a timely manner.

This projection reminded me how vital it is for all of us to remember that ChatGPT is not a replacement for critical thinking, creativity, and human contact.

As instructors, we should allow our students to use ChatGPT as a learning tool, but we should equally advise them not to rely on it. While ChatGPT might provide useful clues, it is not always accurate and lacks the contextual knowledge required to deliver complete responses to assignment questions. Students should be made aware that in order to score highly, they will need to synthesize information from a variety of sources in order to offer relevant and suitable answers. ChatGPT could be part of this where academics have approved its use, but not all of it.

Furthermore, we should make students aware that in order to develop abilities that they can apply in the job, they must learn to think independently and solve problems on their own. Their time in higher education is the time to develop and hone these skills that will serve them for the rest of their lives. It is critical that we begin open dialogues with our students about the usage of ChatGPT in education right away. We can only highlight the benefits and limitations of employing AI technology and encourage students in using them safely and ethically if we engage in open and honest conversation with them.

What Impact Will ChatGPT Have on Education and Teaching?

With all of ChatGPT's possible applications, you might be wondering how it might affect schooling.

Technology has transformed schooling in numerous ways over the years. It has increased kids' and instructors' access to resources, but it has also produced more substantial disparities and diversions in the classroom. For better or worse, technology in the classroom is here to stay, and new technology is being introduced on a regular basis.

ChatGPT was released to the public in 2022 by OpenAI, an artificial intelligence research and development organization. ChatGPT is a free tool that anyone with a device and internet access may use, making it broadly available, particularly for students who are all digital natives at this time.

How can teachers make use of ChatGPT?

1. Additional resource

Consider ChatGPT to be similar to Google, but without the need to go through results. For example, if a teacher is teaching about the Revolutionary War and there is a class discussion on why the war started, Google will provide thousands of results for students to sort through. ChatGPT, on the other hand, would provide a quick, succinct, and straightforward answer that students could read in real-time. ChatGPT can enhance conversations and provide real-time answers to teachers in this fashion.

2. Evaluations

ChatGPT has the ability to generate assessments. Teachers can feed information and context into the AI algorithm, and ChatGPT will generate an output. When constructing assessments from scratch, it might be an excellent beginning point for teachers.

3. Grammar and composition

Grammar and writing might be challenging for teachers to convey to students in the age of social media and text language. ChatGPT gives students quick feedback, which can help them improve their writing skills. While AI should not be used to replace a teacher's lessons, it can be used as a practice tool for teachers in the classroom as well as a means to mix things up and bring something fresh for pupils.

4. Automation

Automation is all around us, and it may help instructors automate one of their most time-consuming tasks: grading. ChatGPT can score and provide feedback on tasks, providing teachers more time to develop engaging lessons and focus on students.

How can students make use of ChatGPT?

1. Assist with homework

Another option that students can use to get quick responses is ChatGPT. You've probably seen students say, "Hey Siri..." after pressing the iPhone button. Siri responds immediately. ChatGPT is a similar concept. ChatGPT can be useful for homework if they need rapid responses that they don't have to comb through.

2. Writing abilities

There are various writing assistance tools available, such as NoRedInk and Grammarly. ChatGPT works in a similar manner. A learner can enter a sentence and request that ChatGPT correct it for them in order to see how it can be improved.

3. Feedback

Because ChatGPT has data analysis capabilities, a student might type an essay into the text box and request feedback from ChatGPT.

This allows the student to make any necessary changes before submitting the assignment. In addition, a student can enter an exam into ChatGPT, and the AI will determine which areas the student needs to improve on.

4. Conduct Research

ChatGPT is very sophisticated and has a lot of resources. However, its database is made up of internet sources, some of which are bound to be erroneous. This indicates that students should use ChatGPT as a source similar to Wikipedia. It can be useful for basic knowledge and as a jumping-off point, but it cannot be used as a citation source.

What are the advantages and disadvantages of using ChatGPT in the classroom?

Some teachers worry that artificial intelligence is out to get them. Others, though, are embracing it as a grading tool and another way to teach students how to engage with technology. Examine the benefits and drawbacks of ChatGPT in education. The following are some of the benefits of using ChatGPT in education.

ChatGPT delivers a wide range of topics in real time, allowing for quick access to information. **Personalized learning:** Students can customize inquiries to their specific interests and even ask follow-up questions so that ChatGPT can go deeper into that topic.

Supplemental resource: By conducting a short search of its database, ChatGPT provides teachers with access to a wealth of knowledge.

Language practice: Students can use the AI program to practice, receive feedback, and ask for assistance.

Accessibility: Teachers must strike a work-life balance, which means they cannot respond to emails at all hours of the night. Students can access ChatGPT for information 24 hours a day, seven days a week, especially when their teacher is unavailable.

Cons

ChatGPT's accuracy is limited because its data is obtained from the internet. The following are some disadvantages of using ChatGPT in education:

Inadequate context: ChatGPT is intelligent, yet it can misinterpret context, resulting in inaccurate output.

Lack of critical thinking: Critical thinking is one of the most valuable skills kids can learn. They will not have to think for themselves if the answers are always at their fingertips.

Lack of originality: ChatGPT may generate entire essays. If a student lets ChatGPT compose their essay for them, they are not only lacking in creative thought; they are also committing plagiarism. This is one of the most serious problems with ChatGPT, and plagiarism checkers are racing to keep up. ChatGPT is trained on data, and if the data is biased, so is the computer.

We've already seen it happen: pupils (and some teachers) can't seem to get away from their phones. Humans become more dependent on technology when it is introduced. With such an accessible search engine, it's easy to utilize ChatCPT as a crutch rather than a tool.

ChatGPT's Future in Education

Artificial intelligence (AI) is sweeping the globe. We look at the potential and limitations of AI tools like ChatGPT in education, as well as how you can encounter them in your studies.

The introduction of the AI chatgpt has been sparking widespread interest in mainstream and social media. However, not everyone welcomed its release, with the NSW Department of Education and other districts acting quickly to prohibit its usage in their schools.

So, what does this suggest for the usage of ChatGPT and other artificial intelligence tools at university? We learn about ChatGPT, its limits, and how the University will employ it and other AI tools while retaining academic integrity. For example, if you ask ChatGPT about strategies to restrict the transmission of airborne infections, it will immediately respond with pages of text that it develops specifically for you, citing masks, hygiene, and ventilation. It does this not because it understands your inquiry, but because it has learned that terms like "mask," "cleaning," and "indoor spaces" are likely to appear together, after words like "limit the spread" and "airborne pathogen." ChatGPT is currently available for free trial. It does, however, need you to sign up, agree to its privacy policy, and recognize that you will use it to train the AI.

ChatGPT In the Classroom

As AI technology and tools advance, you will see more of them used in your studies and evaluations. While AI will someday profoundly disrupt the way humans' study, learn, and work, don't expect any significant changes in the near future. For the time being, you can expect to experiment with, as well as discuss and criticize, AI's outputs in your present studies.

AI technologies, like any other resource you utilize in your studies and assessments, should be approached critically, with an honest and authentic recognition of their limitations. In accordance with our academic honesty policies, you should not use ChatGPT or other writing tools in an evaluation unless explicitly permitted. Failure to acknowledge the usage of AI technologies in your studies may expose you to cheating charges. You must acknowledge using these tools in your study if you are permitted to do so.

Expect to hear more from the University, your professors, and your supervisors about how we're addressing the benefits and difficulties that AI brings to higher education. We are constantly trying to protect academic integrity and the value of your degree, while also preparing you to be ethical leaders in a future where these technologies provide new and exciting opportunities.

CHAPTER FIVE

Evaluating Effectiveness of AI Powered Prompts

AI-powered prompts can be evaluated based on their effectiveness in achieving their intended purpose. The effectiveness of AI-powered prompts can be measured through various metrics, such as accuracy, precision, recall, and F1 score. Accuracy refers to the proportion of correct predictions made by the AI-powered prompt, while precision measures the proportion of true positive results among the predicted positive results. Recall measures the proportion of true positive results that were correctly identified by the AI-powered prompt, and F1 score is a combination of precision and recall.

In addition to these metrics, other factors that can be used to evaluate the effectiveness of AI-powered prompts include user satisfaction and the overall impact on the intended audience. User satisfaction can be measured through surveys and feedback mechanisms, while the overall impact can be assessed through various indicators such as increased engagement, improved productivity, or enhanced outcomes.

The effectiveness of AI-powered prompts will depend on the quality of the underlying AI algorithm, the accuracy and relevance of the data used to train the model, and the suitability of the prompts for the intended audience and context. Evaluating the effectiveness of AI-powered prompts requires careful consideration of these factors and ongoing monitoring and refinement to ensure optimal performance. When evaluating the effectiveness of AI-powered prompts, it's important to consider the specific use case and the intended audience. For example, if the AI-powered prompt is designed to help users complete a specific task, such as booking a flight, the effectiveness of the prompt can be evaluated based on metrics such as the completion rate, time taken to complete the task, and user satisfaction.

Accuracy is another important metric for evaluating the effectiveness of AI-powered prompts. In the case of a chatbot or virtual assistant, accuracy refers to the ability of the AI-powered prompt to understand and respond to user queries correctly. Precision and recall are also important metrics for evaluating the effectiveness of AI-powered prompts in the context of classification tasks, such as identifying spam messages or detecting fraudulent transactions.

User satisfaction is an important factor to consider when evaluating the effectiveness of AI-powered prompts. Users are more likely to continue using a product or service if they find it easy to use and helpful. User satisfaction can be measured through surveys, feedback mechanisms, or user engagement metrics such as the number of interactions per user or the time spent on the platform.

The overall impact of AI-powered prompts on the intended audience is also an important factor to consider. For example, if the AI-powered prompt is designed to improve productivity in the workplace, the impact can be measured through metrics such as the time saved, the number of tasks completed, or the overall efficiency of the organization.

Measuring the Effectiveness of AI in the Modern World

An AI system's output is not an end in itself. This indicates that the success of an AI system is determined by its ability to achieve the objectives of the mission supported by the system while utilizing the system's output. This is manifested in the context of intelligence by the fact that no matter how self-contained any given AI system is, its output will contribute to informing intelligence assessments. These evaluations provide decision makers with knowledge about the globe that they can use to make decisions that influence the security of the United States.

The impact of the actions chosen is the ultimate cause of success or failure for the AI system. In an ideal world, the system's success would be understood by following the impacts backward through this chain of consequences. That is, each change in the United States' security position would be traced back to decisions made by decision makers, which in turn would be linked back to the intelligence used to select those actions, all the way back to the system's output. In this manner, the system would be judged based on the net influence it had on the outcome we care about the most directly: the general security of the United States.

Unfortunately, when such systems are examined in the context of intelligence, effectiveness is not so easily defined and assessed. Intelligence cannot be measured in dollars and cents. In a 2016 ODNI whitepaper titled "Processes for Assessing the Efficacy and Value of Intelligence Programs," for example, it is stated that "the efficacy of any particular program is difficult to assess," in part because individual programs "are not typically used in isolation."

A thorough examination of the challenge of evaluating the success of the intelligence process or current ODNI evaluation policy is much beyond the scope of this report, and we do not intend to comment on the relative utility of this approach. However, it should be noted that the approaches provided in this white paper do not directly quantify the effectiveness of program reporting. To put it another way, the mechanism described by ODNI examines whether consumers are satisfied, not the impact of the reporting.

If decision makers had to pick between a program that produced reports that were regularly quoted and satisfied intelligence consumers and one that significantly boosted US security, they should go with the latter. These measurements are thus helpful primarily as a proxy for the favorable effect on US security, which is more difficult to quantify.

Indeed, we require such proxies because tracing this effect back to the system is complicated and would necessitate understanding how reporting influences analysts, how those analysts influence policymakers, and the concrete impacts of policymakers' actions on US security and interests. This final step appears extremely difficult, as it would necessitate a thorough understanding of geopolitical evolution to support an analysis of how the world would have altered if US officials had taken a different path.

On"Human Equivalent" Performance

For systems that replicate a task currently performed by humans, there is always one minimum standard of performance available to decision makers considering the deployment of an AI system: the performance of the system in question can be compared to that of the humans currently performing the task. For example, in a task where humans might reasonably be expected to disagree on some examples, such as assessing the objectivity of an intelligence product, the AI system performing the task can be judged by whether it is at least as good as the average human performing the task at predicting the majority opinion. This criterion is a suitable baseline for system performance to demand before deployment if this system is being evaluated for deployment to save time or effort on the part of the humans currently executing the task.

Though the specific hazards are unknown, the risks taken by deploying the system are the same risks accepted by the existing process that employs humans to accomplish the activity. While this approach is feasible, it has significant limitations, including the inability to estimate impacts other than the resources required to perform the task at a given degree of risk. There are stronger and weaker techniques to compare the performance of AI systems to determine which one is better.

To put it another way, exceeding human performance needs the AI system to perform better regardless of which errors are more serious. However, depending on which errors are more serious, AI systems may perform better than or equal to human performance in "impact-adjusted" terms, even if not significantly better. Furthermore, just because a human and a machine make errors at the same rate does not guarantee that they will make the same errors.

Consider a system that recognizes automobiles in photos as an example. It is likely that the characteristics of a given image that cause people to struggle with the task differ from those that lead machines to struggle. Humans may struggle to detect automobiles in photographs with inadequate illumination, whereas machines may struggle with crowded images. If a certain class of photos is especially significant, such as photographs with bad lighting circumstances, then human comparable performance must be specified in a finer-grained manner that distinguishes between performance on distinct classes of images. Of course, in order to make this fine-grained distinction, a reproducible description of the many classes of images of varying relevance is required.

These faults may also not be dispersed in time in the same way. For example, if more than one person collaborates with another to complete a task and these persons work in shifts, error rates may change between shifts since we should expect some people to be more effective at the activity than others.

Evaluation Support System

Evaluation support systems are those whose output is employed in the intelligence cycle's evaluation stage. In other words, these are systems whose output is used to monitor the intelligence process, assess how effectively it is working, and recommend areas for improvement. The 2016 ODNI whitepaper, for example, emphasizes in the preface that "for reasons of feasibility and effectiveness, these methods [that count the citations of reports in intelligence products] focus on reports and citations that fit carefully defined criteria." A computer system might be used to assemble and analyze these counts at scale. It would be an evaluation support system if such a system were constructed.

Similarly, one could envision developing a system to aid or partially automate the review of finished intelligence products, such as by using natural language processing (NLP) to score each finished product for objectivity, one of the five analytic standards outlined in "Intelligence Community Directive 203: Analytic Standards."14 A system like this would also be an evaluation assistance system.

Evaluation of present procedures and efficacy is an important part of the feedback loop that IC uses to make improvements, reforms, and reinvestments. As a result, inaccuracies in an evaluation support system's output may influence decisions about which programs to extend and which to cut, who to promote and who to lay off, and where the greatest value from new programs and innovations may lie.

Unfortunately, these implications are inextricably linked to the challenging topic of measuring the intelligence process's overall performance. As a result, it appears that systems in this category cannot be examined for direct impact without addressing that question in some way. However, when examining specific evaluation support systems, the features of the system's deployment context may give a means to systematically identify and model consequences in a way that falls short of tracing the impact all the way to the actions chosen by policymakers.

Automated Analysis System

Automated analysis systems change or enrich data without human intervention to aid intelligence analysis just like the chatgpt. Informally, an automated analysis system is any system that makes conclusions from intelligence data. The important element of these systems is that, while they employ intelligence data to determine what they offer to their consumers, they modify it in some way rather than simply presenting the complete dataset. An automated analysis system would be one that crops out and displays only the most relevant portion of an image that has been annotated with additional context.

These systems can help with the intelligence cycle's processing, analysis, production, and dissemination processes. The system envisioned by IARPA's MATERIAL program, for example, would be an automated analysis system. This program contributes to efforts to develop "English-in, English-out" information retrieval, which returns relevant materials in other languages as well as English summaries of these papers that include the relevance of the documents to the query. When the user cannot understand the language in which the document is written, the English summary may stand alone as capturing the contents of the document.

Collection Assistance Systems

Collection support systems are those whose output directs or initiates the gathering of new intelligence. In other words, these are systems whose output influences where a camera is pointed, where an Intelligence, Surveillance, and Reconnaissance drone flies, or which new lead is forwarded to a case officer. As a result, collection support systems must support functions in the intelligence cycle's planning and direction or collecting stages. Collection support systems and information prioritizing systems share many similarities at the most fundamental level of analysis.

Because a sensor cannot point everywhere at once, these systems select what it does and does not point at. If the sensor fails to generate relevant information, the sensor's time has been lost in the same manner as an error in an information prioritization system wastes user time. Similarly, the reporting that originates from the program guided in part by the collection support system determines the return on investment of "sensor time."

Why Effective Prompts are Important for Writing

A writing prompt is a cue given to someone to help them recollect ideas for writing or what they're going to say. It is frequently a scribble of ideas and thoughts in the shape of paragraphs, open-ended sentences, a theme, or a setting that prompts writing. As an example: A cue is something like whispering a few words to an actor who has forgotten their next line. Another example is providing an author a sentence and having them develop a story around it; the sentence given is a prompt. A prompt that says, "If you're stuck, write about it." I leaped up and did a happy dance, relieved that my writing prompts had come to my aid. As is customary.

Creators are sometimes struggling for ideas, face writer's block, or are left looking for a source of inspiration. At times, individuals simply want to put themselves to the test or explore a new genre. Writing prompts are a tried-and-true method for dealing with problems like this. It is frequently used synonymously with scribbling or journaling.

Writing prompts, often known as timed essays, are learning tasks that direct or "prompt" students to write about a given topic in a specified manner. Prompt writing is a long-standing and effective method of teaching writing composition because it encourages students to focus on a specific issue, idea, or concept and to express their own ideas on the topic presented by the prompt. Prompts encourage students' critical thinking and allow them to develop a reasoned and structured argument in response to another writer's point of view.

Effective writing prompts are important because they help writers overcome writer's block, generate new ideas, and develop their writing skills. Writing prompts can come in many forms, such as a sentence or a question, an image, a piece of music, or a video. They can be used for various purposes, such as to stimulate creativity, encourage exploration of a topic, or develop a specific writing skill.

One of the most significant benefits of effective writing prompts is that they encourage creativity. A good writing prompt should be open-ended enough to allow for different interpretations and approaches, while also being specific enough to give the writer a starting point. When writers are presented with a writing prompt, they are encouraged to think beyond their usual thought patterns and explore different ideas and perspectives.

Writing prompts also help writers to develop their writing skills. By providing a structure and framework for writing, prompts can help writers to practice different types of writing, such as descriptive, narrative, or persuasive writing. Effective prompts can also help writers to develop specific writing skills, such as improving their grammar, syntax, or vocabulary.

Writing prompts can also be used to encourage exploration of a topic. Effective prompts can present a topic in a new way or from a different perspective, challenging writers to think outside the box and develop fresh ideas. This can be particularly useful for writers who are struggling to generate ideas or who are looking to develop their writing in new directions.

Writing prompts offer variety. Effective prompts can provide writers with a range of topics to choose from, which can help to keep writing fresh and interesting. This is particularly useful for writers who work on long-term projects or who write on a regular basis, as it can help to prevent burnout and keep them motivated.

Effective writing prompts are crucial in helping writers develop their skills and craft. A writing prompt is a starting point, often in the form of a question, statement, or image, that encourages a writer to begin writing. It serves as an inspiration for the writer, helping them to overcome writer's block, develop their ideas, and create a structured piece of writing. The following are some reasons why effective writing prompts are important for writing:

Encourages Creativity: Writing prompts can spark the imagination and encourage creativity in the writer. By providing a starting point, a prompt allows the writer to explore different ideas and themes. This can lead to unexpected and innovative writing that may not have been possible without a prompt.

Provides Focus: Writing prompts provide a specific topic or theme to explore. This can help writers focus their writing and prevent them from becoming overwhelmed by too many ideas. By narrowing down the topic, a writer can develop a more cohesive and relevant piece of writing.

Offers a starting point: Sometimes, writers may have an idea but may not know where to start. A writing prompt provides a starting point for the writer, making it easier for them to begin writing. This can help writers who struggle with writer's block or those who are intimidated by a blank page.

Encourages exploration: Effective writing prompts can encourage writers to explore topics that they may not have considered before. By presenting a topic in a new way or from a different perspective, a prompt can challenge writers to think creatively and develop fresh ideas.

Develops writing skills: By providing a structure and framework for writing, prompts can help writers develop their writing skills. This includes improving grammar, syntax, and vocabulary, as well as developing a clear and concise writing style. Writing prompts can also help writers to practice different types of writing, such as persuasive writing, narrative writing, or descriptive writing.

Offers variety: Writing prompts can provide writers with a variety of topics to choose from. This can be particularly useful for writers who work on long-term projects or who write on a regular basis. Having a range of prompts to choose from can help to keep writing fresh and interesting.

CHAPTER SIX

Examples of AI-Powered Prompts

A I-powered prompts are generated by artificial intelligence systems that are designed to assist humans in various tasks. These prompts are based on machine learning algorithms that analyze large amounts of data and identify patterns and trends. These algorithms can then make predictions or suggestions based on the data they have analyzed. AI-powered prompts can be used in many different contexts, including writing, marketing, customer support, finance, creativity, productivity, health, language learning, travel, and education. Let's take a closer look at some of these contexts.

In writing, AI-powered writing assistants can suggest words, phrases, or even complete sentences to help writers overcome writer's block or improve their writing. These writing assistants can analyze a writer's style and suggest alternative phrasing or synonyms that may better fit their writing style or intended message. In marketing, AI-powered marketing platforms can suggest keywords, ad copy, and other marketing messages based on consumer trends and behavior. These platforms can analyze consumer data, such as browsing and purchase history, and identify patterns that can inform marketing strategies and tactics.

In customer support, AI-powered chatbots can suggest responses to customer inquiries based on a database of commonly asked questions and answers. These chatbots can also use natural language processing to understand the context of a customer's inquiry and provide more personalized and relevant responses. In finance, AI-powered financial assistants can suggest investment options or identify potential savings opportunities based on a user's financial data and goals. These assistants can analyze a user's income, expenses, and investment history to make personalized recommendations that align with their financial objectives.

In creativity, AI-powered creativity tools can suggest ideas for artwork, music, or other forms of creative expression. These tools can analyze patterns in existing works and identify potential themes or motifs that a user may wish to explore in their own work. In productivity, AI-powered productivity tools can suggest task priorities, reminders, and other tips to help users stay on track and improve their efficiency. These tools can analyze a user's workflow and identify areas where they may be able to streamline their processes and work more efficiently. In health, AI-powered health apps can suggest personalized workout plans or dietary recommendations based on a user's fitness data and goals. These apps can analyze a user's biometric data, such as heart rate and activity levels, and make recommendations that align with their health and wellness objectives.

In language learning, AI-powered language learning apps can suggest vocabulary words or phrases based on a user's level and learning style. These apps can analyze a user's progress and identify areas where they may need additional practice or exposure to new vocabulary.

In travel, AI-powered travel apps can suggest travel destinations or activities based on a user's preferences and past travel history. These apps can analyze a user's travel patterns and interests to make personalized recommendations for their next trip. In education, AI-powered educational platforms can suggest learning materials or study resources based on a student's learning style and progress. These platforms can analyze a student's performance and identify areas where they may need additional support or resources to succeed.

AI-powered prompts can be a valuable tool for improving efficiency, productivity, and effectiveness across a wide range of contexts. By leveraging the power of machine learning algorithms, these prompts can help humans make better decisions and achieve their goals more effectively. Here are some examples of AI-powered prompts in various contexts:

Writing: "Write a story about a world where humans live on floating islands above the clouds."

Marketing: "Suggest a personalized product recommendation for a customer who recently purchased a book on cooking."

Customer Support: "Suggest a response to a customer who is asking for assistance with resetting their password."

Finance: "Suggest a savings goal for a user based on their income and expenses."

Creativity: "Suggest a color palette for a user who is designing a new website."

Productivity: "Suggest the most important task to complete next based on a user's current workload."

Health: "Suggest a new workout routine based on a user's fitness goals and activity level."

Language Learning: "Suggest a list of vocabulary words for a user who is learning Spanish at an intermediate level."

Travel: "Suggest a travel destination for a user who is interested in beach vacations and has a budget of $1,000."

Education: "Suggest a quiz or worksheet for a student who is studying for a history exam on World War II."

Strategic Examples of Prompts from various Field of Life

Music

❖ Write a song about a feeling of nostalgia. Think about a time in your life that was particularly meaningful or special to you. Consider the emotions you felt during that time and try to capture those feelings in your lyrics and melody. Use descriptive language and vivid imagery to help your listeners connect with the song on a deeper level.

❖ Create a playlist for a road trip with your best friends. Consider the mood and tone of the road trip, as well as the tastes and preferences of your friends. Think about the types of music that will get everyone excited and energized, and include a mix of old favorites and new discoveries. Consider adding some songs that everyone can sing along to, as well as some hidden gems that will surprise and delight your friends.

❖ Write a jingle for a new product launching soon. Think about the product's unique features and benefits, as well as the target audience. Consider the mood and tone of the jingle, and try to create a catchy melody and memorable lyrics that will stick in people's minds. Focus on the product's key selling points and try to convey these in a fun and engaging way.

❖ Compose a piece of music that represents the four seasons. Think about the different moods and feelings associated with each season, as well as the sights, sounds, and smells that are unique to each one. Consider the instrumentation and tempo of the music, and try to create a piece that captures the essence of each season while also flowing seamlessly from one to the next.

❖ Write a song about the struggles of being a teenager. Think about the challenges and pressures that teenagers face, such as peer pressure, identity issues, and academic stress. Consider the emotions and experiences that come with these struggles, and try to create a relatable and empathetic song that will resonate with teenagers and adults alike.

Excel sheets:

❖ Create a budget tracker for your monthly expenses. Think about the different categories of expenses you have, such as housing, food, transportation, and entertainment. Consider the frequency and amount of each expense, and create a spreadsheet that tracks your spending over time. Use formulas and charts to help you analyze your spending patterns and identify areas where you can cut back.

❖ Develop a sales report for your business for the last quarter. Think about the key metrics that are important to your business, such as revenue, profit, and customer acquisition. Consider the different channels through which you generate sales, such as online sales, in-store sales, and partnerships. Create a spreadsheet that tracks these metrics over time, and use charts and graphs to help you visualize your progress.

❖ Create a project timeline with milestones and deadlines. Think about the different stages of the project, such as planning, execution, and evaluation. Consider the tasks and deliverables associated with each stage, and create a timeline that outlines the key milestones and deadlines. Use conditional formatting to highlight upcoming deadlines and track progress against your timeline.

❖ Develop an inventory management system for your warehouse. Think about the different types of inventory you have, such as raw materials, finished goods, and work-in-progress. Consider the flow of inventory through your warehouse, and create a system that tracks inventory levels, orders, and shipments. Use formulas and conditional formatting to help you manage inventory levels and identify potential shortages or surpluses.

❖ Create a data analysis spreadsheet to track employee performance metrics. Think about the key performance indicators that are important to your business, such as sales revenue, customer satisfaction, and employee retention. Consider the different departments and roles within your organization, and create a spreadsheet that tracks these metrics for each employee. Use pivot tables and charts to help you analyze the data and identify trends and patterns over time.

Designers:

❖ Design a new logo for a startup company in the technology industry. Research the company's mission, values, and target audience, and create a logo that reflects these elements while also being modern and visually appealing. Consider the use of color, typography, and symbolism to make the logo memorable and recognizable.

❖ Create a user interface design for a mobile app that helps people track their daily water intake. Consider the user experience and how to make the app easy to navigate and use. Incorporate gamification or other engaging features to encourage users to drink more water. Consider the use of graphics and animations to make the app visually appealing and engaging.

❖ Design a package for a new brand of organic food products. Research the target audience and consider the brand's values, such as sustainability and health. Incorporate natural and earthy tones to reflect the organic nature of the products, and consider using eco-friendly materials for the packaging. Make the packaging visually appealing and easily identifiable on store shelves.

❖ Create a poster for a music festival featuring multiple artists. Incorporate the festival's branding and theme into the poster design. Consider the use of typography and imagery to make the poster eye-catching and memorable. Incorporate the different artists and genres into the design while maintaining a cohesive overall look.

❖ Redesign the website of a local restaurant to make it more user-friendly and visually appealing. Consider the user experience and how to make the website easy to navigate and use. Incorporate high-quality images of the restaurant's food and atmosphere, and make the menu easily accessible. Use colors and typography to create a visual hierarchy that guides users through the website.

Travel Guide:

❖ Write a guide to the top tourist attractions in a major city. Research the city's most popular attractions and landmarks, and provide information on their history and significance. Include practical information such as admission prices and hours of operation, and provide recommendations for the best times to visit.

❖ Create an itinerary for a two-week trip to a foreign country. Consider the traveler's interests and preferences, and include a mix of cultural, historical, and outdoor activities. Provide practical information such as transportation and lodging options, and include recommendations for local cuisine and entertainment.

❖ Write a guide to the best restaurants and bars in a popular tourist destination. Research the city's culinary scene, and provide information on the best restaurants and bars for different types of cuisine and atmospheres. Include practical information such as hours of operation and price ranges.

❖ Create a guide to the best hiking trails in a national park. Research the park's trails and provide information on their difficulty level, length, and scenic views. Include practical information such as trailhead locations and any necessary permits or fees.

* Write a guide to the best beaches in a tropical paradise. Research the beaches and provide information on their amenities, such as parking, restrooms, and beach rentals. Include information on the water temperature and any safety concerns, and provide recommendations for local restaurants and attractions.

Event Planners:

* Plan a corporate event for a company's annual meeting. Consider the company's goals and objectives for the event, and create a theme and overall vision. Plan the event timeline, and coordinate logistics such as catering, audio-visual, and transportation.

* Create a budget and timeline for a wedding ceremony and reception. Work with the couple to determine their vision for the wedding, and create a budget that accommodates their needs and preferences. Develop a timeline that outlines all necessary preparations and includes deadlines for vendors and other suppliers.

* Plan a charity fundraiser for a local nonprofit organization. Work with the organization to determine the fundraising goals and create a theme and vision.

Health and Wellness:

❖ Design a workout program for a client looking to improve their overall fitness. Consider their goals, fitness level, and any health or mobility issues. Create a program that includes a mix of cardio, strength, and flexibility exercises, and provide instructions on proper form and progression.

❖ Develop a meal plan for a client looking to lose weight and improve their overall health. Consider their dietary restrictions, preferences, and lifestyle, and create a plan that includes a mix of nutrient-dense foods and healthy snacks. Provide recommendations for portion sizes and timing of meals.

❖ Write a guide to stress management techniques for busy professionals. Provide information on the physical and mental effects of stress, and offer practical techniques for reducing stress, such as meditation, exercise, and time management. Provide examples of how these techniques can be incorporated into a busy schedule.

❖ Create a mindfulness program for a group of seniors in a retirement community. Consider their physical limitations and cognitive abilities, and create a program that includes gentle movement, breath work, and guided meditation. Incorporate activities that promote social connection and engagement.

❖ Develop a mental health program for a college campus. Consider the unique challenges faced by college students, such as academic pressure and social isolation, and create a program that promotes mental health and wellness. Offer resources such as counseling services, support groups, and self-care workshops.

Sports:

❖ Develop a training program for a high school athlete looking to improve their performance in their sport. Consider the demands of the sport and the athlete's position, and create a program that includes strength and conditioning exercises, sport-specific drills, and flexibility training. Provide instructions on proper form and progression.

❖ Write a guide to the rules and regulations of a popular sport. Provide information on the objective of the game, scoring, and penalties. Include diagrams and illustrations to help explain key concepts, and offer tips for strategy and technique.

❖ Develop a coaching philosophy for a youth sports league. Consider the developmental needs of the athletes, and create a philosophy that emphasizes sportsmanship, teamwork, and fun. Provide guidelines for practice and game management, and offer resources for parent education and support.

❖ Write a guide to sports nutrition for young athletes. Provide information on the nutritional needs of young athletes, and offer practical tips for pre- and post-game meals and snacks. Include recipes for healthy snacks and meals that are easy to prepare and transport.

❖ Develop a program for athletes returning from injury. Consider the physical and mental challenges of returning to sport after an injury, and create a program that includes rehabilitation exercises, sport-specific drills, and mental skills training. Provide resources for emotional support and guidance on injury prevention.

Politics:

❖ Write a policy brief on a current issue in national politics. Provide background information on the issue, and offer analysis of the potential impacts of proposed policies. Consider the perspectives of different stakeholders, and offer recommendations for action.

❖ Develop a social media campaign for a local political candidate. Consider the candidate's platform and target audience, and create a campaign that includes messaging and visuals that are engaging and persuasive. Consider the use of social media influencers and paid advertising to reach a wider audience.

❖ Write a guide to advocacy for a grassroots organization. Provide information on effective advocacy strategies, such as lobbying, coalition building, and public speaking. Offer resources for developing policy proposals and making presentations to elected officials.

❖ Develop a media strategy for a nonprofit organization working on a political issue. Consider the organization's goals and target audience, and create a strategy that includes messaging, media relations, and social media outreach. Consider the use of traditional media outlets and online platforms to reach a wide audience.

Python:

❖ Write a Python script that uses machine learning to predict the outcome of a sports match.

- ❖ Develop a Python program that can scrape data from a website and store it in a database.

- ❖ Create a Python application that can generate random passwords of varying complexity.

- ❖ Build a Python web application that allows users to search for restaurants based on their location and cuisine.

Buyers and Sellers:

- ❖ Describe the advantages and disadvantages of using online marketplaces for buying and selling products.

- ❖ Write a story about a successful entrepreneur who started as a buyer and eventually became a seller in a particular industry.

- ❖ Analyze the impact of social media on the buying and selling behavior of consumers.

- ❖ Discuss the ethical considerations that buyers and sellers should keep in mind when engaging in transactions.

Personal Life:

- ❖ Write an essay on the importance of personal development and self-improvement in one's life.

- ❖ Discuss the benefits and drawbacks of pursuing a work-life balance.

- ❖ Describe the ways in which travel can enrich a person's life and broaden their perspective.

❖ Write a personal reflection on a difficult experience that taught you an important lesson about life.

Poets:

❖ Analyze the use of imagery and symbolism in the poetry of William Wordsworth.

❖ Compare and contrast the styles of Emily Dickinson and Walt Whitman.

❖ Discuss the role of nature in the poetry of Robert Frost.

❖ Write a critical analysis of a poem by Maya Angelou, examining its themes, imagery, and symbolism.

Prompts on Customer Service

Imagine you are a customer service representative for a large company. You have just received a call from an upset customer who has been experiencing issues with your product or service. Write about your approach to handling the situation and resolving the customer's concerns. Consider the following questions in your writing:

❖ How do you address the customer's concerns and demonstrate empathy?
❖ What steps do you take to investigate and understand the customer's issue?
❖ How do you work with the customer to find a solution that meets their needs?
❖ What actions do you take to follow up with the customer and ensure their satisfaction?

Use this prompt as an opportunity to explore the importance of effective communication, problem-solving, and relationship-building skills in customer service. Consider the impact that positive customer interactions can have on a business, and the ways in which companies can prioritize customer satisfaction as a key metric for success.

How to Modify and Personalize AI Generated Prompts

While AI-generated prompts can be a great starting point for generating ideas, it's important to personalize and modify them to better suit your needs and goals. Here are some tips for modifying and personalizing AI-generated prompts. Modifying and personalizing AI-generated prompts can help you tailor your content to your specific needs and audience. Here are some additional details on how you can modify the generated prompt.

Understand the AI model: It's important to understand the AI model that's generating the prompts. Each AI model has its own unique strengths and weaknesses. For example, some models may be better at generating creative content, while others may excel at providing factual information. Understanding the capabilities of the AI model can help you decide how to modify the prompts.

Identify the areas to modify: Once you understand the AI model, you can identify the areas that need modification. This may involve changing the tone of the prompt, using different vocabulary, or adding specific context or details to make the prompt more relevant to your needs.

Use prompt conditioning: Many AI models allow you to condition the prompts by providing additional information or context. This can help you personalize the prompts based on your needs. For example, you might provide information about your target audience, such as their age, interests, or profession, to help the AI generate prompts that are more relevant to them.

Use templates: Many AI platforms provide templates that you can use to modify the prompts. These templates can serve as a starting point and provide a structure for the prompts. They may include specific fields or variables that you can customize to personalize the prompts.

Review and refine: Once you've modified the prompt, review it carefully to ensure that it meets your needs. This may involve checking for grammatical errors, ensuring that the tone is appropriate for your audience, and verifying that the prompt is relevant to your needs.

Test and iterate: Once you have a modified prompt, test it with your intended audience to see how it performs. This may involve using the prompt in marketing campaigns, social media posts, or other content. Based on the results, you may need to iterate on the prompt and make further modifications to improve its effectiveness.

Identify the main topic or theme: Look at the prompt and identify the main topic or theme that it is addressing. For example, if the prompt is about Python programming, the main topic is coding in Python.

Modify the language and tone: AI-generated prompts may not always be written in a way that is compatible with your writing style or tone. Modify the language and tone of the prompt to better suit your own style and tone. For example, if the prompt is written in a formal tone and you prefer a more casual tone, adjust the language accordingly.

Experiment with different angles: Don't be afraid to experiment with different angles or perspectives on the main topic. Consider how you can approach the topic from a unique angle or bring a fresh perspective to the subject matter. For example, if the prompt is about poetry, you might focus on the intersection between poetry and politics or explore the role of poetry in contemporary culture.

Don't limit yourself to one type of prompt: AI tools can generate a wide variety of prompts, from creative writing prompts to business writing prompts. Don't limit yourself to one type of prompt; explore different types of prompts to see what works best for you and your goals.

By following these best practices, you can use AI-powered prompts to generate high-quality ideas and spark your creativity, while also maintaining control over your writing and staying true to your personal style and goals.

The Future of ChatGPT Looks Promising

As technology advances, more individuals will certainly employ this type of artificial intelligence (AI) to assist them with daily tasks. This encompasses everything from informal talk with friends and family to more sophisticated duties like coordinating many activities at the same time.

ChatGPT bots can be used to automate discussions, which eliminates the need for a user to manually enter text and wait for a response. Instead, based on what it has learnt from past exchanges, the bot will answer automatically with predefined responses. In many cases, this could save time and allow users to focus on more vital duties.

ChatGPT has the ability to completely transform the customer service business. Instead of a human agent, clients could be serviced by ChatGPT-powered AI bots. Because the bot can learn from previous interactions with clients, this allows for faster and more accurate responses. ChatGPT can also assist organizations in automating operations such as data entry, online ordering, and customer assistance. Businesses could save time and money while enhancing efficiency.

The future of ChatGPT appears promising as it continues to evolve and improve. ChatGPT is poised to become a key player in the AI business, with the ability to change the customer service industry and automate monotonous chores.

The possibilities are essentially limitless, and as more firms adopt this technology, we can expect to see even more ChatGPT applications in the future. ChatGPT, for example, can be used to provide more personalized client experiences by enabling tailored interactions based on individual needs. It has the potential to be employed in a variety of other fields, including healthcare, finance, education, and others. We should anticipate to see even more applications for ChatGPT in the future as technology evolves and advances.

Will ChatGPT take over Jobs?

ChatGPT was created to assist businesses in automating client contacts and providing more tailored, human-like experiences. But, with this technology, a significant concern arises: will ChatGPT replace jobs?

The short answer is no. ChatGPT is intended to supplement and not replace existing customer service teams. It allows customer care agents to focus on more sophisticated or critical duties while ChatGPT handles more monotonous or repetitive chats.

ChatGPT enables companies to be more efficient while also providing better customer service. Customers can obtain faster and more accurate responses to their enquiries by automating discussions. Furthermore, ChatGPT is highly customizable, with rules and settings that ensure client happiness.

The AI has the ability to help organizations become more efficient while maintaining a high level of customer service. It is not intended to replace real customer service representatives, but rather to supplement them. ChatGPT, when properly implemented, maybe a valuable asset for firms looking to improve their customer support capabilities.

ChatGPT will not replace your work, but it may help you do it better by enabling faster and more accurate responses in client encounters. So, don't be hesitant to embrace and experiment with new technology; it could make your job a lot easier.

However, Microsoft designed ChatGPT to make it easier for people to create discussions without having to type out every response manually. As a result, many people have begun to employ this technology for personal purposes. But the question remains: is ChatGPT trustworthy?

On the other hand, this question has two answers: yes and no. ChatGPT can be a valuable tool for fast starting conversations, but it's crucial to note that the software cannot think for itself or forecast how others will react in certain scenarios. As a result, ChatGPT exchanges can sometimes sound robotic, and responses may not always make sense in certain scenarios.

ChatGPT, on the other hand, has been significantly improved and is now more reliable than before. The software has been trained on hundreds of millions of real-world talks and can deliver reliable predictions for a wide range of conversations. ChatGPT is also continually updated with fresh information and features, making it an even more dependable option for starting conversations.

It can be a valuable tool for fast tracking conversations, but it's crucial to realize that the software can't think for itself or forecast how others will react in certain scenarios. It is best utilized as a tool to assist individuals quickly develop ideas and inquiries. ChatGPT can be a dependable choice when used correctly.

The significance of ChatGPT's rise stems from how helpful and effective a tool it has shown to be as well as the ways in which it can push the boundaries of what humans can and cannot do.

The AI is not flawless and is still in its early phases of development it is still prone to bias, simple errors, and disinformation, implying that, despite the astounding progress it is spearheading, there is still a long way to go to reach improved accuracy and lower hazards associated with relying completely on it. This underscores the importance of human judgment and knowledge in navigating the results generated by AI, distinguishing between good and bad results, and making the most of its capabilities.

ChatGPT represents a paradigm shift in the efficiency, efficacy, speed, and sustainability of our operations. As more AI-powered tools emerge on the crest of the OpenAI wave, it will not be AI that replaces jobs. Professionals who understand how to use AI tools will replace those who do not adapt and learn to use the power of technologies to their advantage.

With that stated, certain jobs will undoubtedly undergo greater transformation than others, and it is critical to anticipate how the expectations and nature of the jobs most affected will alter.

Conclusion

In conclusion, creating effective prompts is a crucial skill for anyone who wants to engage others in meaningful communication, whether it's in writing, teaching, or any other form of interaction. Effective prompts should be clear, concise, and focused on a specific topic or idea. They should also be relevant to the intended audience, and provide enough context and information to guide them towards a thoughtful response.

To create effective prompts, it's essential to consider the purpose of the prompt, the audience, and the desired outcome. This can involve thinking about the key ideas or concepts that need to be addressed, as well as any potential challenges or obstacles that the audience may face. Additionally, it's important to craft prompts that are open-ended enough to encourage creativity and critical thinking, while also providing enough structure to prevent confusion or ambiguity.

By taking these factors into account, anyone can create effective prompts that inspire thoughtful discussion, encourage reflection and analysis, and ultimately, lead to deeper understanding and engagement. Whether you're a teacher, a writer, or simply someone looking to spark a conversation, the ability to create effective prompts is an invaluable tool that can help you communicate more effectively and connect more meaningfully with others.

AI has evolved to enhance human creativity. It's not about AI taking over the creative field or replacing jobs, but it's more about working together to create and deliver efficiency and better brand engagement. By analyzing data, generating new ideas, and automating repetitive tasks, AI can aid productivity and overall output. It's time to embrace this superhuman technology and see its results in bettering human productivity. AI is becoming ubiquitous and sooner or later it will completely integrate itself into our personal and professional lives and not adapting to its prowess is foolhardy for any enterprise that wants to remain relevant in the near future.

ChatGPT is a still-developing AI technology that, with its powerful and versatile Natural Language Processing tool, has the potential to change the way people engage with technology. Its true potential has yet to be realized. It can be enhanced in areas that are weak with regular updates, as there is continuing research and development in the field of Natural Language Processing, and it is likely to continue to increase the capabilities and performance of these models over time.

Another important aspect of creating effective prompts is to ensure that they are inclusive and sensitive to diverse perspectives and experiences. This means considering the cultural, social, and political contexts in which the prompt will be presented, and avoiding language or topics that may be offensive or exclusionary to certain groups.

Additionally, effective prompts should be tailored to the level of the audience's expertise or knowledge. For example, a prompt designed for a beginner audience will differ from one meant for advanced learners or experts. It's important to use appropriate vocabulary, concepts, and examples that match the audience's level of understanding.

Another strategy for creating effective prompts is to incorporate multiple perspectives or voices. This can help to broaden the scope of the discussion and encourage participants to consider different viewpoints and experiences. For example, prompts could include quotes from experts or diverse community members, or ask participants to consider multiple sides of an issue.

Finally, it's important to allow for flexibility and adaptability in creating effective prompts. Sometimes, the best prompts may come from unexpected sources or arise organically from a conversation or experience. By remaining open to new ideas and approaches, anyone can create effective prompts that foster meaningful dialogue and engagement.

In conclusion, ChatGPT is a powerful language model that can help users achieve maximum results when used effectively. To get the most out of ChatGPT, it's important to consider a few key strategies. First, it's important to provide ChatGPT with clear and specific prompts. The more detailed and focused the prompt, the better ChatGPT can understand the user's needs and provide relevant and accurate responses.

Second, users should take advantage of ChatGPT's ability to learn and adapt to specific needs and preferences. By providing feedback and correcting errors, users can help ChatGPT improve its performance and provide more useful responses over time.

Third, it's important to use ChatGPT as a tool for exploration and discovery. Users can ask open-ended questions and experiment with different prompts to uncover new insights and perspectives.

Finally, users should be mindful of ethical considerations when using ChatGPT. This includes avoiding using ChatGPT for malicious purposes, such as spreading misinformation or harassment. It also means being aware of biases that may be present in the data used to train ChatGPT and striving to create inclusive and diverse prompts and interactions.

By following these strategies, users can use ChatGPT to achieve maximum results and leverage its powerful capabilities to enhance their learning, communication, and creativity.

Recommendations

ChatGPT is designed to provide assistance in a variety of contexts. Here are some recommendations for using ChatGPT effectively:

Be clear and concise in your requests: ChatGPT is programmed to respond to specific questions or prompts. To get the best results, it's important to be clear and concise in your requests. For example, instead of asking a general question like "tell me about science," you could ask "what are the four fundamental forces of nature?"

Use proper grammar and spelling: ChatGPT's responses are based on the inputs it receives. Using proper grammar and spelling can help ChatGPT better understand what you're asking for and provide more accurate responses.

Provide context: When asking a question, it's helpful to provide context so ChatGPT can better understand the scope and intent of your question. For example, if you're asking about a particular topic, provide some background information so ChatGPT can provide more relevant information.

Don't rely solely on ChatGPT: While ChatGPT is a powerful tool, it's not infallible. It's always a good idea to double-check the information you receive and do additional research if necessary.

Be respectful: ChatGPT is programmed to provide helpful responses, but it's important to remember that it's not a human being. Avoid using inappropriate language or making offensive comments when interacting with ChatGPT. following these recommendations, you can make the most of your interactions with ChatGPT and receive more accurate and helpful responses.